W9-DBO-515

As one of the world's longest established
and best-known travel brands,
Thomas Cook are the experts in travel.

For more than 135 years our
guidebooks have unlocked the secrets
of destinations around the world,
sharing with travellers a wealth of
experience and a passion for travel.

Rely on Thomas Cook as your
travelling companion on your next trip
and benefit from our unique heritage.

Thomas Cook **traveller** guides

NORTHERN SPAIN
Suzanne Wales & Mary-Ann Gallagher

Thomas
Cook

Your travelling companion since 1873

Written by Suzanne Wales and Mary-Ann Gallagher
Original photography by Caroline Jones

Published by Thomas Cook Publishing
A division of Thomas Cook Tour Operations Limited.
Company Registration no. 3772199 England
The Thomas Cook Business Park, Unit 9, Coningsby Road,
Peterborough PE3 8SB, United Kingdom
Email: books@thomascook.com, Tel: + 44 (0) 1733 416477
www.thomascookpublishing.com

Produced by Cambridge Publishing Management Limited
Burr Elm Court, Main Street, Caldecote CB23 7NU

ISBN: 978-1-84848-222-7

First edition © 2010 Thomas Cook Publishing
Text © Thomas Cook Publishing
Maps © Thomas Cook Publishing/PCGraphics (UK) Limited

Series Editor: Maisie Fitzpatrick
Production/DTP: Steven Collins

Printed and bound in Italy by Printer Trento

Cover photography: © SIME/von Drachsberg/4CR

Contents

Introduction

'Spain is different'. So states the slogan that was devised to bring visitors to the country in the 1960s – the beginnings of an industry that has become one of the country's main money-spinners. Nearly 50 years on it is still cited, often referring to the country's inherent 'exoticism' or certain cultural quirks. But, as a generic bucket-and-spade tourism has proliferated in the southern part of the peninsula, it's the north that has retained this exciting (and enticing) 'difference'.

Yet still, with the exception of Catalunya, 90 per cent of foreign visitors to Spain eschew the north in favour of the south. For the tourist who is happier to discover ancient cities, tread along a mountaintop or taste the celebrated cuisine of Northern Spain, this is good news. Travellers here will find a less jaded welcome, in fact most will be overwhelmed by the enthusiasm Northern Spaniards have for sharing knowledge of their land and culture. A strong love of nature and sense of place unites these peoples, whose ancient ancestors battled tooth and nail against the Moorish settlement of Spain. While nationalistic sentiment was forcibly repressed during General Franco's dictatorship (1939–1975), it came bouncing back after his death and the rebirth of democracy. All Spanish regions now enjoy an unprecedented (at least for the modern era) amount of autonomy, which has revitalised local cultures and languages and created a heady melting pot of diversity and respect.

If local pride unites Northern Spaniards in character, a green, mountainous landscape physically unites this swathe of Spain. The mountains are rarely out of view in this part of the country, be they the snow-capped peaks of the Pyrenees, the craggy Sierra de la Demanda in La Rioja or the limestone massifs of the Picos de Europa in Cantabria and Asturias. Architecturally, a common thread has been provided by the 'Camino a Santiago' (The Santiago Way). As this great Christian pilgrimage gathered momentum, monasteries, churches and hospitals were erected to accommodate (and attract) the pilgrims, from simple squat Romanesque churches to soaring Gothic cathedrals and monasteries, such as the Santiago de Compostela Cathedral in Galicia and the Leyre Monastery in Navarra. Bold contemporary architecture is also a feature of these regions, a sign of its new economic stability and investments in the arts. Bilbao's Guggenheim Museum has been hailed as the greatest building of the 20th century, and a new arts complex by architect Oscar Niemeyer – the grandfather of modernist architecture – will put the tiny Asturian town of Avilés on the map. The wine region of Álava boasts a clutch of exciting new wineries designed by internationally renowned architects, a brave bid that has kick-started wine tourism in the region.

But Northern Spain will also delight with its smaller pleasures, ones that lie away from the main cities and designated 'tourist routes'. Crisp weather and verdant valleys coax the growth of an abundant number of vegetables that are sold in the weekly open-air markets of nearly every village you will stumble across, where farmers pour down from the mountains to sell their produce. Watching local fishermen haul in their catch in the villages along the coast is an experience perhaps only matched by eating it in the local restaurant the same evening. After this, you may like to join the locals in the main square as they sip drinks and chat about the day's events, smug in the knowledge that they live in a privileged pocket of the world. These are the experiences that will make your trip to Northern Spain memorable – and cherished for time to come.

The arid plateaux of Bardenas Reales

Land and people

Northern Spain is a loose term, covering areas that in some cases have no clear geographical boundaries. For the purposes of this book we have included the regions of Galicia, Asturias, Cantabria, La Rioja, Navarra, Euskal Herria (or Basque Country) and the upper swathes of Catalunya and Aragón; all of which have their own distinct character. Diversity is the adjective that most describes Spain, and this is particularly true of the north, cradle of the principalities, dukedoms and kingdoms that once constituted the land we now call 'Spain'.

In the Middle Ages, these regions successfully fought tooth and nail against the Moorish occupation of the peninsula, and some tribes even resisted the Romans, resulting today in an infallible identity and rich thread of unique traditions. Their peoples will always describe themselves by provenance first (Galegos, Catalan, Euskaldunak (Basque), etc.) and 'Spanish' second. Each region has its own language or languages, be it an official one that lives alongside Castilian Spanish (which is spoken all over the country) or a dialect that has survived in an isolated mountain community. Culturally, you will find influences of Celtic tradition in Galicia, Provençal French in Catalunya, and Basque in the Basque country and Navarra.

The Pyrenees and Picos de Europa mountain ranges form a massive wall across Northern Spain from Catalunya to Asturias. Older than the Alps, the Pyrenees are divided into three sections – Western, Central and Eastern (the

latter of which forms a natural border with France) – and they are at their highest in the Vall d'Aran in Catalunya, where the Pico de Aneto rises up over 3,400m (11,150ft). They are marked by a frequency of mountain torrents and waterfalls and cirques (round valleys formed at the head of the glacier by erosion). Wild flowers often dot meadows of the upper peaks, and forests, proliferated by frequent rain and sheer isolation, clad the sides of many of the mountains. Birds of prey – especially eagles, vultures and falcons – are a common sight.

The Eastern Pyrenees give way to the Picos de Europa in Cantabria and Asturias, the largest national park in Europe. The *picos* are characterised by limestone mountain peaks (many of them more than 2,500m/8,200ft high), caves, beautiful meadows and valleys, and stunning views (the range is located a mere 15km/9 miles inland from the Cantabrian coastline). The 'elusive' brown bear that inhabits these parts is

Land and people

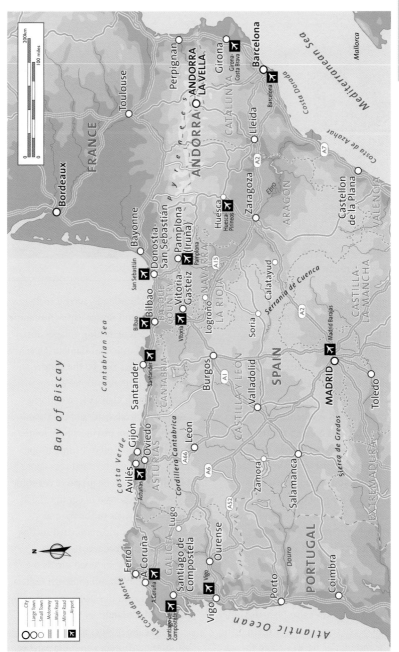

Vegetable garden in Hecho village, Aragonese Pyrenees

becoming slightly less so (37 cubs were born in 2008), and sightings of chamois are common on the upper peaks.

Unlike many parts of the south, tourism is not the mainstay of Northern Spain. Historical events aside, one reason is the weather. Sub-zero temperatures can be felt in mountainous areas in winter, and Galicia is covered in mist or rain for a good part of the year. Even in the summer you would be wise to be prepared for cold nights (and even cool-ish days), and the weather can change very rapidly.

Another factor is its coast. For the most part, it is devoid of the long stretches of sandy beach that characterise Southern Spain – and hence (blessedly) also high-rise hotels and beach resorts. In Northern Spain the mountains have touched the sea

with cliffs, headlands, surreal rock formations and savage capes. Authentic and picturesque fishing villages dot both the Atlantic and Cantabrian coasts and the sea has shaped the culture and livelihood of their peoples for centuries, particularly in Galicia (the nation's supplier of fresh fish) and the Basque Country, whose mariners have long held the reputation of being Europe's finest. Enticing, protected coves are plentiful, though be prepared for some icy waters (yes, even in summer) and large waves; parts of the Basque coastline are world-renowned surfing destinations. More resort-type destinations are scattered across the gentler Rías Baixas in southern Galicia, a beautiful coastline criss-crossed with rivers and wetlands.

Despite the proliferation of astounding churches and monasteries, religion doesn't play as big a role in Northern Spain as you may think. While 75 per cent of Spaniards identify themselves as Roman Catholics, only 19 per cent attend church every Sunday. Even the religious pilgrimage, the Camino a Santiago, which is plotted across a huge chunk of Northern Spain west of Navarra, is undertaken as much for the glorious scenery it provides as for any religious significance. That is not to say that religion is not present in everyday life; most traditions here have their roots in religion, usually honouring the patron saint of the village. But like most gatherings in Spain, they take on a festive air where people from young to old and all walks and creeds participate – an endearing trait that is 'typically' Spanish.

Land and people

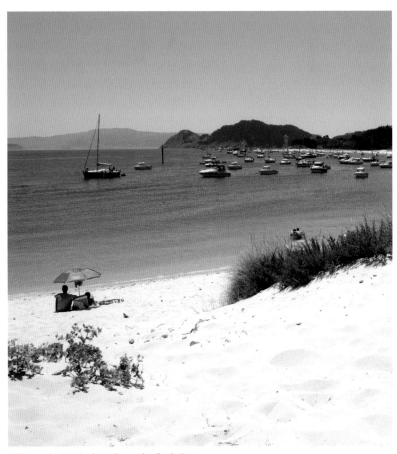

White sands at Praia de Rodas on the Illa de Faro

History

c. 16,000–9,000 BC Magdalenian hunter-gatherers occupy numerous caves throughout Northern Spain, particularly in Cantabria and Asturias. These early humans have left extraordinary artworks, particularly in the Cueva de Altamira.

1200 BC The Celts begin to arrive on the Iberian Peninsula, gradually integrating with local Iberian tribes. The Celts build fortified settlements called *castros*, the remains of which still survive in Galicia, Asturias and Cantabria.

202 BC With the culmination of the Second Punic War, the Romans wrest control of the Iberian Peninsula from the Carthaginians. The Romans remain in Iberia for the following five centuries, but find the remote northwestern regions and their troublesome tribes difficult to control.

5th century AD The Western Roman Empire is crumbling, and Germanic tribes take advantage of its weakness. Vandals, Alans, Suevi and Visigoths sweep across the Pyrenees, looking to expand their territories, but are resisted by local tribes. The Visigoths left the strongest influence in Northern Spain, particularly in the architecture.

711 Muslim Arab armies cross the Straits of Gibraltar and sweep up through the Iberian Peninsula. They are stopped by a Frankish army at Poitiers in 732, and are forced back across the Pyrenees. Nonetheless, most of the peninsula is under Arab control by the end of the 8th century. Local Christian nobles retreat to their mountain strongholds.

722 The Arab defeat at the Battle of Covadonga in 722 by the Asturian lord Pelayo is often described as the beginning of the *Reconquista* (Reconquest). (In reality a minor skirmish, which would later take on retrospective historical significance and become an intrinsic part of Spanish national mythology.)

813 The relics of St James are discovered in Santiago de Compostela by the bishop Theodomir, and veneration of the saint develops into an international cult.

1212 The Arab armies are defeated by a Christian alliance at the Battle of Las Navas de Tolosa (in present-day Andalucía). The northern kingdoms take advantage of the weakness of Al-Andalus to expand their boundaries.

1469 The marriage of Isabella of Castilla and Ferdinand of Aragón, 'the Catholic Kings', signifies the first major stage in the unification of Spain. Navarra is annexed in 1512, and Granada, the last Muslim kingdom in Spain, falls in 1492.

1492 Christopher Columbus makes his first voyage to the New World, initiating the development of the Spanish Empire. Many sailors and explorers came from Northern Spain, notably Juan Sebastián Elcano, a Basque, who was the first to circumnavigate the globe (in 1521).

1516–56 Under the rule of the first Habsburg king of Spain, Carlos I (also Charles V, Holy Roman Emperor), Spain's territories in Europe and the New World are vastly expanded. However, Carlos I proclaims that all trade is to pass through Seville, to the detriment of the ports on the northern coast and in Catalunya.

1635–59 Spain is at war with France. The war is concluded with the Treaty of the Pyrenees (1659), by which Spain is forced to cede territories in Northern Catalunya.

1700 Carlos II, the last Habsburg king of Spain, dies without an heir, sparking off the first War of the Spanish Succession (1701–14). The Basque Country and Navarra support Felipe V, of the French Bourbon dynasty, and are rewarded when he is victorious. Catalunya and Aragón, however, are punished for supporting his rival, and are stripped of their historic rights and privileges. After the war, Seville's monopoly on trade with the Americas ends, resulting in an economic boom in Northern Spain.

1808	Napoleonic armies invade Spain and kidnap the Spanish royal family, triggering the Peninsular War. Ferdinand VII is deposed and Joseph Bonaparte (Napoleon's brother) is made king in his stead. The French are defeated in 1814, and Ferdinand VII is reinstated.
1833–76	The death of Fernando VII without an heir in 1833 sparks off the Carlist Wars, which continue erratically until 1876. The worst conflicts take place in Northern Spain, and the Basque town of Bergara serves as the Carlist base and court. Alfonso XII is crowned king in 1876.
Second half of the 19th century	Nationalist sentiment grows throughout Northern Spain. This movement is particularly intense in Catalunya, the Basque Country and Galicia. Industrialisation continues apace, but tensions between wealthy factory-owners and poverty-stricken workers grow.
1898	Spain loses its last overseas possessions in the Spanish-American War. The country becomes increasingly destablised.
1923–30	In the face of political and social turmoil, General Miguel Primo de Rivera declares himself dictator, with the support of Alfonso XIII, the army and the Roman Catholic Church.
1931–6	Primo de Rivera resigns in 1930, and the Republicans win municipal elections in 1931. The Second Spanish Republic is declared. Alfonso XIII abdicates, and a new Constitution is signed. This establishes the right of all of Spain's regions to autonomy, a right which Catalunya and the Basque Country immediately exercise.
1936–9	A left-wing coalition wins the Spanish general election in 1936. The result is disputed by the right-wing

opposition, and civil war breaks out. General Franco leads the Nationalist armies against the Republicans in a brutal conflict that culminates with Franco's victory in 1939.

1959 The Basque terrorist organisation ETA (Euskadi Ta Askatasuna) ('Basque Homeland and Freedom' in Basque) is founded in response to Franco's repression of regional identities. ETA doesn't begin its campaign of armed struggle until the 1960s.

1975 Death of Franco. A new Constitution is signed, and the Spanish regions are given limited autonomy. ETA is not satisfied, and the late 1970s are marred by more than 300 fatalities.

1986 Gesto por la Paz ('Association for Peace in the Basque Country') is founded; it hosts silent demonstrations against violent killings.

1992 Olympic Games are hosted by Barcelona. Some events are held in Puigcerdà and La Seu d'Urgell in the Catalan Pyrenees.

1997 The Guggenheim Museum opens in Bilbao.

2002 The oil tanker *Prestige* sinks off the Galician coast, causing Spain's worst ecological disaster.

2004 Terrorist bomb attacks on Madrid trains result in 191 deaths. The government blames ETA, even after it becomes apparent that the attack was carried out by an extremist Islamic group, and it loses the general election a few days later. The incoming socialist government led by José Luis Rodríguez Zapatero is perceived to be more sympathetic to regional calls for more autonomy.

2006 Catalunya's Statute of Autonomy is revised, but the Catalan request to describe their region as a 'nation' provokes furore throughout Spain.

2009 ETA threatens to kill those involved in the building of the new Basque high-speed train line.

2016 Donostia-San Sebastián is a candidate city for European City of Culture.

Politics

Spain is a constitutional monarchy, with a king (King Juan Carlos I) and a parliament known as the Cortes Generales led by an elected prime minister (currently José Luis Zapatero). Modern democracy is relatively new to the country. After the death of General Franco in 1975, Spain went through an upheaval and rebirth known as la transición *(the transition), which decentralised Spain and gave political autonomy to its 17 diverse regions (known as* communidades autónomos*).*

There are two leading national parties in Spain: the centre-right Partido Popular (PP) (Popular Party) and the left-of-centre Partido Socialista Obrero Español PSOE (Spanish Socialist Workers Party). In autonomous community elections, local parties often align themselves with either one.

Galicia

Galicia is often perceived as the most conservative of Spain's autonomous communities. General Franco was a Galegos (born in the city of Ferrol) and until 2005 Manuel Fraga, a member of Franco's old regime and founder of the Partido Popular, presided over the Xunta, Galicia's autonomous government. For the next four years, the Xunta was governed by the PSOE. In 2009 the PP won the elections.

Asturias and Cantabria

The Principality of Asturias was the first kingdom to be established in Iberia after the defeat of the Visigoths in the early 8th century. Under Franco, and his endeavour to wipe out regional nationalism, it was simply named 'Province of Oviedo'. Cantabria, like Asturias, also lost its historical autonomy under Franco's dictatorship. In both regions, local government today is headed by the PSOE.

La Rioja

The second smallest of Spain's autonomous communities, La Rioja's future independence was in much discussion during *la transición*, when they considered incorporating it into Castilla y León or the Basque Country. On 9 June 1982, a Statute of Autonomy was ratified, an event celebrated every year on La Rioja Day. The PP is the ruling party.

Navarra

Navarra was once a kingdom in its own right and stretched to present-day La Rioja, the Basque Country, Cantabria and parts of Aragón. Today it is known as a *communidad foral*, enjoying special governmental rights such as defining and managing its own tax system. The northern part is more akin to the Basque Country both culturally and politically (Basque is widely spoken), and nationalist spirit is strong. It is governed by the Unión del Pueblo Navarro (UPN) (Navarran People's Union), a conservative regional party.

Aragón

Aragón was also a kingdom in its own right, born in the northern valleys of Echo and Cafranc in the 8th century, and at its height encompassed Catalunya and Navarra. Even before Franco's death, underground organisations had made steps to organise self-government, and during *la transición* Aragón was a pioneer in creating its own statute. It is governed by a coalition of the PSOE and Partido Aragonés (PAR) (Aragón Party), a centre-right nationalist party.

Basque Country (Euskal Herria)

Nationalism marks every facet of Basque politics. Nationalist parties claim that the constitution creating autonomous communities was forced upon them, and the terrorist group ETA and its handful of political arms (many of which are officially banned) want nothing less than secession from Spain. In 2009, after 30 years of nationalist rule, the role of Lehendakaritza (Basque presidency) was transferred to the more moderate Euskadiko Alderdi Sozialista-Euskadiko Ezkerra (PSE-EE) (Basque Socialist Party), marking a new direction in Basque politics.

Catalunya

Nationalism is also strong in Catalunya, particularly in the north, the ancient strongholds of Catalunya's count-kings. The Generalitat (local government) was presided over by the centre-right, nationalist Convergència i Unió (CiU) (Convergence and Union) party until 2003, a period in which Catalunya received ever-expanding autonomy and Catalan once again became the lingua franca. Today it is governed by the Partit dels Socialistes de Catalunya (PSC) (Socialist Party of Catalunya) in coalition with nationalist, left-leaning Esquerra Republicana de Catalunya (Republican Left) and Iniciativa per Catalunya Verds (ICV) (Initiative for Catalonian Greens) – a unique situation known as the *tripartite* (three-party rule).

The Ikurriña (Basque flag)

Politics

Culture

The area covered in this guide encompasses eight very distinct Spanish regions, each with its own culture and history and even, in many cases, its own language. Northern Spain can offer visitors everything from Celtic legends in Galicia to dynamic 21st-century architecture in La Rioja, and from superb Paleolithic artworks in Cantabria to the extraordinary, thousand-year-old pilgrim path of the Camino a Santiago.

Architecture

Each region of Northern Spain covered in this book is unique in terms of history and culture, and this is reflected in the architecture. In Galicia, for example, stone is widely used as a building material because of the damp climate; Santiago de Compostela has been called a 'symphony in stone', and its graceful balustrades and cupolas – made of marble or tiles in other cities – are beautifully carved from Galician granite. The stone granaries, called *hórreos*, which are propped on stilts to prevent rodents from entering, are still a common sight. In the remote peaks of the Picos de Europa, Asturian shepherds still spend the summer months in *teitos*, the traditional thatched huts that accommodate livestock on the ground floor and shepherds on a sleeping platform above them. In the Basque Country and Catalunya, the sturdy stone country houses (*masía* in Catalan and *etxe* in Basque) functioned not simply as homes, but also farms, fortresses and an assembly point for locals. Many of these country homes have now been converted into comfortable rural hotels, a delightful way to experience the traditional architecture at first-hand.

As well as vernacular architecture, Northern Spain is notable for its outstanding legacy of pre-Romanesque and Romanesque architecture. The pre-Romanesque churches of Oviedo (Asturias) are astoundingly beautiful, and technically astonishingly advanced for the age. The scores of exquisite Romanesque churches that dot almost every Catalan Pyrenean village are similarly spellbinding and provide a window into a crucial era in medieval history, when the battle between the local Christians and the Muslim armies from North Africa was at its height.

The 21st century has seen a marked shift towards the age of the celebrity architect. Frank Gehry's landmark building for the Guggenheim Museum in Bilbao, which opened in 1997, was the first in a long line of ambitious architectural projects that have mushroomed across Northern Spain. These include a huge arts complex by Oscar Niemeyer in Avilés (still under construction) and a slew of designer *bodegas* in the La Rioja wine region, such as the Ysios winery by Santiago Calatrava; Frank Gehry's titanium complex for Marqués de Riscal; and Basque architect Iñaki Aspiazu's zinc and glass cube for the Baigorri winery. Yet more ambitious projects are planned, notably in Bilbao, which has transformed itself almost beyond recognition from the rundown industrial city it was just a couple of decades ago.

Art

Some of the most spectacular ancient artworks ever discovered come from the Cueva de Altamira in Cantabria, described as the 'Sistine Chapel of Paleolithic art' (*see p56*). It is one of several painted caves in Asturias and Cantabria that have been recognised by UNESCO for their outstanding beauty. In the 20th century, the Basque Country produced two extraordinary artists, who would achieve international acclaim: Jorge Oteiza (1908–2003) and Eduardo Chillida (1924–2002). Both were famous for their monumental, abstract sculptures and their pride in Basque culture. Their artworks can be found in major art collections around the world, or you can see their vast public sculptures in cities across Northern Spain, particularly Donostia-San Sebastián, the city most associated with both artists.

The 16th-century citadel in Jaca

Culture

Folklore and legend

Undoubtedly, the greatest single charm of Northern Spain is its exceptional natural beauty. It remains a largely rural region, and agriculture and fishing are still important industries. Life has changed surprisingly little in many of these villages over the last several hundred years, and the old legends still linger. Many stories have been Christianised, but their roots stretch back long before the arrival of Christianity. This is particularly true in Galicia, which is often called the 'Ireland of Spain'. Its Celtic history is still evident in the *cruceiros* (Celtic crosses) found at crossroads, and in the symbols which adorn the local

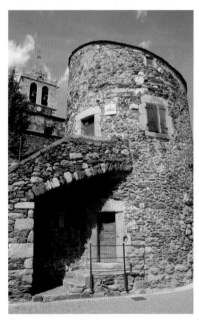

Church and tower, Llivia

architecture. Legends and fairy tales abound in this misty land that is still, so locals will enjoy telling you, peopled with witches, fairies (known as *donas*, *mouras* or *damas*) and a host of strange creatures including goblins and werewolves. The Celts also left their imprint on Asturias and Cantabria, where *xanas* (fairies) are said to inhabit the woods, singing by the streams as they comb their hair. Trees, particularly the oak and the yew, still have a special significance, and have generated numerous legends. In the Basque Country, ancient legends about the old Basque gods still linger. The most important Basque goddess was Mari, a beautiful woman who was said to inhabit caves and gorges. Gradually, her cult was conflated with that of the Virgin Mary, but she continues to be venerated in age-old customs. It was long believed that witches inhabited the remote Basque mountains, which led to a witch-hunt by the Inquisition in 1610 (*see p97*). A witch museum in the Navarrese town of Zugarramurdi offers a glimpse into the world of the wise woman in 17th-century Spain.

Religion

Although the pre-Christian cultures of Northern Spain are still apparent in the region's ancient legends and folkloric traditions, Christianity has shaped Northern Spain most intensely. In the Middle Ages, it was these mountain strongholds that sheltered the Christian nobles as they prepared their armies for

19

Culture

Portal at the Iglesia de Santa María in Deba

the *Reconquista* – the battle to beat back the Muslim armies from North Africa and reconquer the Iberian Peninsula. The ancient churches, monasteries and shrines established across the mountainous north functioned not simply as a celebration of Christianity, but also as a means of consolidating territory by repopulating lands taken from the Arabs.

But perhaps the single greatest contribution by Christianity to Nothern Spain is the Camino a Santiago. The apparent discovery of the relics of St James (Santiago) in the 'field of stars' ('Compostella' is a corruption of the Latin *Campus Stellae*) in Galicia transformed Northern Spain. A small local cult developed into an internationally famous pilgrimage site rivalled only by Rome and the Holy Land. The Camino a Santiago (Way of St James) was born. Pilgrims flooded in from across Europe, and Santiago de Compostela was transformed into a glittering city replete with fine monuments. The towns and villages along the pilgrimage routes also prospered, and even vied to erect monuments which would attract pilgrims. After falling into neglect for several centuries, the Camino a Santiago has recently been revived and attracts tens of thousands of pilgrims annually.

Festivals

There is always something going on in Northern Spain, with fiestas celebrating everything from patron saints to cheeses. You can run with the bulls in Pamplona or hurl jugs of wine in Haro, join in with folk dances in the Picos de Europa or tuck into traditional foods in tiny Galician villages. Local tourist information offices can provide full details of what's on, and regional websites and Spain's official tourism website (www.spain.info) are another excellent resource.

Traditional festivals

Every July, bulls come hurtling down the narrow streets of Pamplona in one of the most celebrated festivals in Northern Spain. Better known outside Spain simply as 'The Running of the Bulls', the Fiestas de San Fermín is held in honour of the local patron saint (*see p88*). In Santiago de Compostela, Santiago (St James) is venerated on 25 July in another huge, city-wide festival, and San Sebastián (patron of Donostia-San Sebastián) is celebrated each January in the deafening drum parade called the Tamborrada. The Fiesta de la Virgen Blanca in Vitoria-Gasteiz is a massive week-long party honouring the 'White Virgin', patroness of the city. These may be the best-known events in Northern Spain, but every town and village celebrates its own patron saint during the annual Fiesta Mayor. These are always colourful, exuberant affairs in which the whole town participates.

If you are in Northern Spain in December, take a stroll around the Christmas fairs, where locals pick up characters to adorn their *belenes* (nativity scenes), an intrinsic part of traditional Spanish Christmas decorations. Children don't receive their presents until the 6th of January, when *Los Reyes* (the Three Kings) parade through towns. Carnival (six weeks before Easter) is not celebrated with quite as much gusto as in Southern Spain, but there are big parades in all major towns. In Alsasua (Navarra), Momotxorros – men wearing terrifying masks and bloodstained costumes – tear through town frightening everyone in an age-old Carnival tradition (*www.alsasua.net*). Easter is usually a solemn affair, but in Avilés (Asturias) there are regattas along the river. There are night-time fireworks across the region for the Fiesta de San Juan on 23 June.

Cultural festivals: Cinema, music, performing arts

The most glittering event in the social calendar in Northern Spain is the San Sebastián International Film

Festival (Donostia Zinemaldia in Basque), held in September (*www. sansebastianfestival.com*). The Basque Country is the place to be for jazz fans in July, with outstanding festivals held in Donostia-San Sebastián (*www. heinekenjazzaldia.com*) and Vitoria-Gasteiz (*www.jazzvitoria.com*). Santander (Cantabria) hosts a superb festival of performing arts (Festival Internacional de Santander) every summer, with music, dance, opera and theatre performances (*www. festivalsantander.com*).

Food and drink festivals

Northern Spain celebrates all manner of food and drink in hundreds of festivals. Almost every town and village has some local product it likes to showcase. For example, in early March, Arzua (Galicia) celebrates its cheese festival (Festa do Queixo), and the famous peppers of Padrón get their own festival in August (Festado Pemento). September is a wonderful month to visit La Rioja wine region, when the harvesting of the grapes is celebrated with countless local fiestas, particularly in Logroño. In Haro, a wild wine battle (Batalla del Vino) takes place in June (*see p104*), and you can try the wonderful Ribeiro wines in Ribadavia's Feria del Vino del Ribeiro held in late April and early May. There are countless cider festivals in Asturias, but the biggest is the Festival de la Sidra Natural in Gijón, which is held in August, and the Festival de la Manzana (apple festival), held in the cider capital of Villaviciosa in October.

Fiesta de La Sacramental in Colombres, Asturias

Highlights

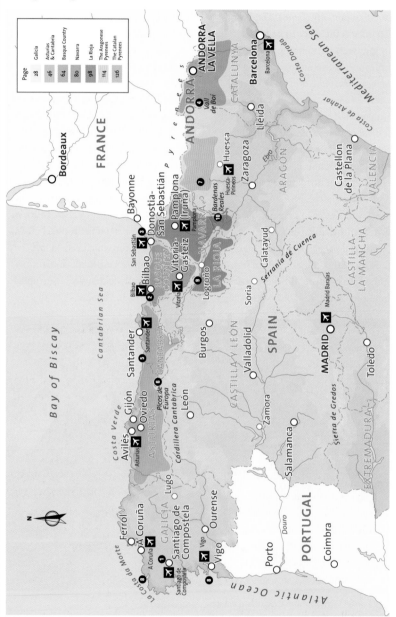

Page	
28	Galicia
46	Asturias & Cantabria
64	Basque Country
80	Navarra
98	La Rioja
114	The Aragonese Pyrenees
126	The Catalan Pyrenees

❶ Santiago de Compostela Discover the bewitching medieval city of Santiago de Compostela, the final destination for the thousands of pilgrims who have trodden the Camino a Santiago. But whether you have travelled hundreds of miles on foot or taken a taxi ride from the airport, the impact of the 'symphony in stone' is the same, particularly when standing at the threshold of Santiago's magnificent cathedral (*see p41*).

❷ Bilbao's Guggenheim Museum It's been more than a decade since the world watched in wonder as architect Frank Gehry unfolded his giant sheets of glittering titanium over Bilbao's murky Nervión river. Since then, Bilbao's Guggenheim has garnered plenty of ink – mainly about modern architecture's ability to put a middling city on the map. The formula has been copied by others cities, but Gehry's Guggenheim remains the leader of the pack and never fails to astound (*see pp66–7*).

❸ Donostia-San Sebastián Eat your way through San Sebastián. The city's reputation as a foodie destination is unequalled anywhere in Europe, with three three-star Michelin restaurants, countless revered others and a frenetic tapas scene. This jewel of the Bay of Biscay could have easily stepped straight off the pages of a romantic novel, with its belle-époque architecture, perfect crescent-shaped beach, elegant promenade and aristocratic airs and graces (*see pp70–73*).

❹ The Romanesque churches of Vall de Boí Between the 10th and 12th centuries, scores of exquisite Romanesque churches with their characteristic slender bell towers were built in the mountains and valleys of the Eastern Pyrenees. The finest of these can still be found on a comfortable drive through the serene valley of Boí, which contains the greatest concentration of Romanesque art anywhere in the world (*see pp132–3*).

❺ Cueva de Altamira Follow in the footsteps of Marcelino Sanz de Sautuola. In 1879, the local amateur archaeologist was walking in the Cantabrian mountains with his nine-year-old daughter, when they discovered an extensive cave covered with breathtaking paintings of bison and other animals. The paintings date from between 16,000 and 9,000 BC and are among the most sophisticated and beautiful ancient artworks ever discovered (*see p56*).

❻ Picos de Europa Hike the soaring peaks of the Picos de Europa. Protected as a national park and recognised as one of Spain's most celebrated natural wonders, the mountains are a paradise for walkers and climbers, and the dramatic gorges, rushing rivers and flower-flecked meadows are home to otters, golden eagles and the elusive brown bear (*see p59 & pp62–3*).

❼ Monasterio de San Juan de la Peña Venture high into the mountains of Aragón to see a monastery hidden from the outside world for centuries. Partly excavated into the side of a rock, San Juan de la Peña is a relic from an age of hermit monks and feudal kings, and is believed to have been the hiding place of the Holy Grail. Its exquisite cloister features some exceptional carvings that fascinate with their eloquence (*see pp118–19*).

❽ Costa da Morte and the Illas Cíes Galicia's Costa da Morte ('Death Coast') delivers breathtaking coastal scenery and secret coves, charming working fishing villages and sublime sunsets from Fisterre ('Land's End'), Spain's easternmost point. Further south, the three-island archipelago of the Illas Cíes is a haven for birds and has exceptional isolated beaches (*see pp30–31*).

❾ La Rioja's Wine Country Drink your way through La Rioja. Wine lovers should not miss Spain's

most productive – and attractive – viniculture country. The Álava region of La Rioja mixes showstopper wineries with ancient underground *bodegas* and majestic monasteries. The food is superb, whether from a cutting-edge restaurant or simple village bar where the region's eponymous drop never stops flowing (*see pp112–13*).

❿ Bardenas Reales Be enthralled by this desert's sheer strangeness. The terrain is a dreamscape of gypsum cliffs and terraces, mountains and mudflats, dotted with prickly juniper bushes and desert flowers. Utterly isolated, eerily silent and constantly battered by the winds of time, the Bardenas Reales is an unforgettable experience (*see pp80–82*).

A detail from the cloister at the Monasterio de San Juan de la Peña

Suggested itineraries

The regions covered in this book cover a vast area of Spain, and each one is a destination in its own right. For shorter trips, travellers would be advised to choose one that corresponds with their interests. For gastronomy, the Basque Country, for wine, La Rioja, or for walking, the Asturias-Cantabria region or northern Aragón would be good bets. Two, or even three, regions could be toured by those in a car on longer trips. Those using public transport and on limited time should not be too ambitious – many remote destinations see only one or two buses a day, and trains only service the major towns.

Long weekend

Travellers coming to Northern Spain for three or four days should choose destinations serviced by an airport with international connections. In Galicia, flying to either A Coruña's or Santiago de Compostela's airport would allow you to see both these enthralling cities comfortably in a few days, with a possible side trip to the Costa da Morte, which starts a short drive south of A Coruña. Bilbao's wonderful airport – designed by the world-renowned Valencian architect Santiago Calatrava – is a hop, skip and a jump from the Frank Gehry's famed Guggenheim Museum (the first distinguishable sight on approach to the city), and a regular bus service connects the city to Donostia-San Sebastián in about 40 minutes. Don't forget to book well ahead if you plan to treat yourself to one of Donostia's famed Michelin restaurants, such as Arzak (*www.arzak.info*) or Martín Berasategui (*www.martinberasategui.com*).

In Catalunya, by hiring a car at Barcelona airport, you can get to the exquisite Vall de Boí – with its famed Romanesque churches – in about four hours and then drive through the beautiful Vall d'Aran (*see 'Drive', pp140–41*).

In Asturias, international flights arrive at Oviedo, the capital of the region. After exploring the city's recently spruced-up historic centre, visit Gijón, slightly further north on the coast, a cheerful port town surrounded by some great beaches.

One week

Lovers of wine could hire a car in Madrid's airport, then merrily spend a week visiting the wineries of Álava, the epicentre of La Rioja's wine production. The first stop would be La Rioja's capital, Logroño, and the tourist office (to pre-book your tours).

Or why not see the north on a train? Dubbed the 'miniature Orient Express', the Transcantabrian (*Apr–Oct only, www.transcantabrico.feve.es*) chugs for eight days along the spectacular coastline of the Cantabrian Sea, from Ferrol in Galicia to Bilbao in the Basque Country,

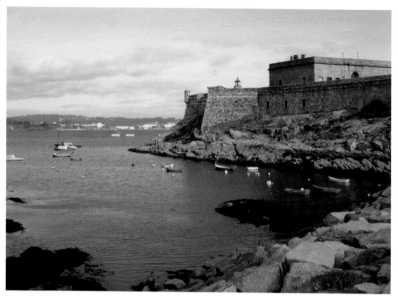

Castelo de San Antón, A Coruña

taking in top destinations such as Gijón, Santillana del Mar and Santander. (From Bilbao passengers can also take a journey inland back to León in Galicia). A local train service (*www.feve.es*) covers much of the same route.

In the same region, walkers could have a splendid week trundling along the peaks of the glorious Picos de Europa, with time left over to visit the 'Sistine Chapel of Paleolithic art', the Cave of Altamira. In Aragón, in the awe-inspiring Ordesa Natural Park, walkers can either take gentle trails using Torla as a base or venture deeper north into Góriz, the location of one of the park's few *refugios* (shared accommodation shelters, *www.goriz.es*). Góriz is the base for climbing Monte Perdido, the highest mountain in the valley.

Two weeks

Two weeks is enough time to explore various aspects and experience the nuances of your chosen region or even two regions. Slowing down will also allow you to act more like a local and really enjoy activities, like partaking in a two-hour lunch, doing some unhurried shopping in a local market or just sitting in a café and watching the world go by.

Many gastronomes would claim that two weeks is not enough to try the culinary delights of Donostia, though outstanding food – whether in fancy restaurants or local village bars – is to be had all over the Basque Country. Its close proximity to Álava, La Rioja's wine country, means that food lovers can have the best of both worlds.

Though not as diverse, the seafood cuisine of Galicia is equally memorable, particularly in the simple eateries of the fishing villages along the coast. Two weeks is ample time to explore Galicia's coastal area, from the Costa da Morte in the north to the Rías Baixas in the south, with a side trip to the heavenly, bird-populated Illas Cíes.

The main roads throughout the Pyrenees are surprisingly well paved and easy to drive. In a few weeks you could explore them from east to west, starting in the lush green valleys of Navarra and then crossing over to the more rugged, higher peaks of Aragón (where you can detour slightly further south to the Romanesque monastery of San Juan de la Peña) and end the trip in Catalunya.

Longer trips

The 'piece of string' adage wholly applies to Northern Spain. With such a diverse range of scenery, cuisine and cultures, and countless notable villages and cities, no matter how long you stay here you will probably always come away craving more. The ultimate discovery route is the Camino a Santiago (*see pp32–3*), a 900km (560-mile) journey starting in the far north of Navarra and ending in Galicia's Santiago de Compostela. For that, all you need is a good pair of walking shoes – and time.

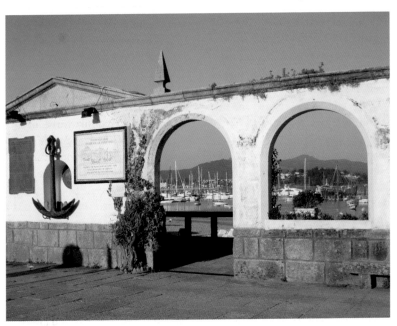

The harbour at Baiona in Galicia

Galicia

Whatever your preconceived notions of Spain are, put them out of your mind when you arrive in Galicia. This northwestern pocket has more in common with the wet and woolly valleys of Ireland or Scotland than it does with the rest of the country. In the lost-in-time rural villages you are likely to hear the sound of the gaita *(Galician bagpipes), and the region's awesome coastline – the epicentre of Galicia's all-important fishing and maritime industry – is lashed by the Atlantic for most of the year.*

Galicia is home to a mere 2.78 million people (less than the population of Barcelona), with the majority living along the Atlantic coastline between Ferrol and Vigo. Galicia's isolation from the rest of the peninsula and economic and cultural ties to the sea, and the hardships that accompany this, have marked its history, though today the region is on the up: the global clothing giant Inditex (creator of the Zara fashion chain) was born here, and the region's two great commodities – wind and unpopulated land – have lead to a booming wind power industry (you will see graceful white turbines dotted all over the landscape). The capital of Galicia is the inland city of Santiago de Compostela, an ancient, glorious city, final destination of the Camino a Santiago pilgrimage, and a must-see for anyone visiting the region.

A Coruña

Once you get past the industrial periphery, you'll find this large port city a fine place to spend a day or two. Located on a natural harbour, A Coruña (La Coruña in Spanish) has always been an important port, first for the Celts, then the Phoenicians and Romans. A Coruña has retained a robust, salty and slightly haughty feel; it wears the riches born by its long maritime history well.

Harbour and headland

The best place to start exploring A Coruña is the maritime road, an elegant boulevard that snakes around the headland and is lined with handsome 19th-century town houses sporting hanging white balconies and glass-enclosed *galerías*. Follow it all the way up to the Castelo de San Antón, an 11th-century castle that today accommodates the city's **Museo Arqueolóxico** (*Tel: 981 18 98 50. Open: Jun–Aug Tue–Sat 10am– 9pm, Sun 10am–3pm; Sept–May Tue–Sat 10am–7.30pm, Sun 10am– 2.30pm. Closed: Mon. Admission* *charge*). Once back down on the sea road, hop on the tourist tram (runs daily) for a jaunt to the Atlantic side of the promontory and the Torre de Hércules, A Coruña's landmark. Dating from the 2nd century (local folklore says that Hercules himself hauled the bricks into place), it is the oldest functioning Roman lighthouse in existence and was recently declared a UNESCO World Heritage Site.

Cidade Vella (Old Centre)

The heart of the Old Centre (and the location of the tourist office) is the arcaded Praza María Pita, named after the feisty heroine who rallied the townsfolk in defence of an attack from Sir Francis Drake's armada in 1507. There is a spear-branding statue of her in the middle of the square. From here, the cobblestoned warren of the Old Centre lies to your east: a charming, often crowded network of noble town

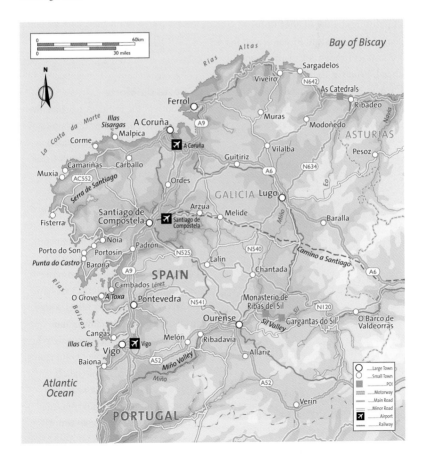

houses, charmingly retro shops (including a puzzling number of shoe shops) and squares. Sites to seek out include the Romanesque **Colexiata de Santa María do Campo** (*Praza Santa María 1. Open: Tue–Fri 9am–2pm & 5–7pm, Sat 10am–1pm. Free admission*), which holds an impressive museum of religious art, and the **Museo de Belas Artes** (*Rúa Zalaeta. Tel: 981 22 37 23. Open: Tue–Fri 10am–8pm, Sat 10am–2pm & 4.30–8pm, Sun 10am–2pm. Admission charge*), which has a handful of paintings by the likes of Rubens, Tintoretto, Goya and Picasso (who lived for a short time in A Coruña as a child). While in the Old Centre, take a break in **Bonilla a la Vista** (*Rúa Real 54*), a city institution famous for its *chocolate con churros* and perfect *patatas fritas* (french fries).

Torre de Hércules, A Coruña

PERCEBES

While you may be drooling at the mussels, crab, octopus, razor clams and other *mariscos* (or shellfish) on display in the window at Galicia's restaurants, you may wonder what those ugly brown barnacle-type critters are and just why they are the most expensive thing on the menu. *Percebes* (goose barnacles) are the king of seafood in these parts and their price is justified by the dramatic way they are gathered. These creatures grow only on the sides of cliffs or rocks thrashed by crashing waves. *Perceberos* lower themselves down, often on ropes after the wave has broken, an incredibly dexterous manoeuvre that you may see as you travel along the Costa da Morte. And the taste? Most compare them to an oyster or simply to 'that of the sea'.

La Costa da Morte

Due south of the capital A Coruña, the coastline from the village of Malpica as far as the cape of Fisterra is known as the Costa da Morte – the 'Death Coast'. Criss-crossed with rivers, dotted with sleepy fishing villages, cradled by the low-rise Sierra de Santiago and blessed with the sort of wild scenery that makes you want to break out in spontaneous applause, it's an exhilarating part of Galicia. Its name is derived from the sheer number of shipwrecks that have occurred in its whipping waves. Stone crosses dot the jagged cliffs in their memory, almost as common a sight here as ancient *hórreos* (elevated grain stores) are throughout the rest of Galicia.

Whitewashed **Malpica** is a lively fishing town that overlooks the Illas Sisargas, home to a large colony of gulls. The fine shell-shaped Area Maior

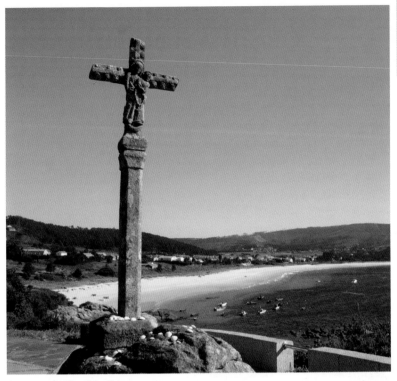

A cross overlooking Cabo Fisterra

beach is just south of the village, while in Malpica itself it's worth seeking out the Romanesque Iglesia de Santiago de Mens.

Other notable stops along the Costa da Morte include **Corme**, situated on a headland where the beaches are wilder and less crowded (Praia Ermida is a good choice), and **Camariñas**, a postcard-perfect village famous for its local lace makers. You can see their work at the **Museo do Encaixe** (*Praza de Insuela 57. Tel: 981 73 70 04. Open: mid-Jun–mid-Sept Tue–Sat 11am–2pm & 5–8pm, Sun 11am–2pm & 5–7pm;* *mid-Sept–mid-Jun Tue–Sat 11am–2pm & 4–7pm, Sun 11am–2pm & 4–6pm. Admission charge*). **Muxía** is less picturesque, but it's worth heading to the tip of the headland and the wave-beaten Santuario de Nuestra Señora de la Barça.

You'll see a few hardy pilgrims making their way over the windswept cape to **Fisterra** ('Land's End'), the very last (and, for most, optional) stop on the Camino a Santiago (*see pp32–3*). Spain's most westerly point, it has an attractive lighthouse and a bar from which to enjoy the magnificent sunsets over the Atlantic.

Camino a Santiago
(The Santiago Way)

One regular sight in Galicia, and indeed over a huge swathe of the territory covered in this book, is the sight of pilgrims. Their backgrounds and nationalities are as diverse as their ages, and whether they have started their journey in France, Navarra or Aragón, their destination is the same: the city of Santiago de Compostela.

Drawing in tens of thousands of people a year, the Camino a Santiago is a huge pull in Northern Spain and

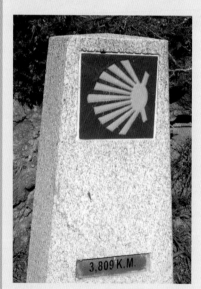

A Santiago waymarker

was probably the country's first exercise in mass tourism. It all started with a legend. In 813 a Galician shepherd received a heavenly calling that guided him to a tomb in the location of the present-day cathedral of Santiago de Compostela. A local priest deemed the cadaver to be that of St James himself (Santiago in Spanish). Just why the apostle James was milling around Spain in the first place has never been properly explained. But with the Moorish occupation of the peninsula steadily edging northwards, the story, however debatable, added ballast to the Christian faith and the *Reconquista* of Iberia.

News of the discovery spread fast throughout Christendom. The first pilgrims arrived from France, crossing into Spain at the mountain pass of Roncesvalles (*see p92*). Over the next centuries, hostels and way stations were set up for them along the way. The *camino* was the impetus for building not only Santiago de Compostela's glorious cathedral but also those of Pamplona (*see p91*) and León, along with countless castles, monasteries, bridges, churches and the distinctive stone crosses you see scattered all over Northern Spain. The route also became a magnet for opportunists, beggars and assorted low-life from the Middle Ages. The French monk Aimery Picaud warned of them in his 12th-century script *Codex Calixtinus*, a sort of early guidebook for the pilgrims. (Roaming wolves were another peril.)

After dropping off the radar through the turmoil of world wars and then Spain's dictatorship, the Santiago Way grew in popularity again in the late 20th century. Old pilgrim hostels were dusted off and reopened, and brass scallop shells (the symbol of the saint) were inlaid into the pavements of towns and villages on the route, 'guiding' pilgrims to their holy destination.

Pilgrims on the route near Castildelgado

Today there are nine official starting points inside Spain from which to embark on the Camino a Santiago (though the 780km/485-mile Roncesvalles, or 'French Route', remains the most historically significant). Pilgrims have to complete 100km (62 miles) of the journey in order to receive the official certificate of completion from Santiago de Compostela's cathedral, their endurance proven by stamps given from Santiago-certified churches and hostels along the way. It would be naive to think that modern-day pilgrims take the journey for religious motives alone, though you will see many that don the traditional pilgrim garb of black cape and staff. The scenery along the route is for the most part breathtaking, and with an abundance of glorious art and architecture and a well-organised network of accommodation and restaurants, it's an enticing option for a walking or cycling holiday – and some echo medieval pilgrims by taking the route on donkey or horseback. Millions are expected to converge in Santiago de Compostela on 25 July 2010, the designated Saint's Day of the next Holy Year.

The Roman bridge in Ourense

Lugo

Capital of Galicia's largest province, Lugo is a fascinating city, one of only two in Spain to have preserved her Roman walls almost entirely intact (the other is Ávila in Castilla y León). You can stroll along the rooftop walkway (built wide enough to fit chariots) of this 2km-long (1¼-mile) wonder with fat medieval watchtowers (known as A Mosquera), admiring the rich ensemble of Gothic, Baroque and Roman structures that lie neatly and compactly within.

Lugo's cathedral is an imposing structure, started in the 7th century but with the usual (for Spain) additions over the centuries. Its highlights are the cloisters and a wide-eyed wooden sculpture of the Virgin set in a Baroque chapel. From here, meander over to the Praza Santo Domingo, and the Gothic-Romanesque convent of the same name with interesting tombs embedded into its walls. Lugo's most famous secular building is the high-Baroque town hall, just near the shaded, spacious Praza Maior. Apart from the walls, Lugo's Roman relics include the lovely **Casa de los Mosaicos**, the remains of a Roman villa with some intricate mosaics in situ (*Rúa Doctor Castro 22. Tel: 982 25 48 15. Open: Tue–Sun 11am–2pm & 5–7pm; Jul–Aug until 8pm. Admission charge*) and the Roman Bridge across the Miño river to the east of the centre.

Ourense and the valleys of Miño and Sil

The Miño river is Galicia's longest river, snaking 307km (191 miles) from the north of the region through Lugo (*see above*) and south along the Portuguese border to the Atlantic. The area southeast of Ourense is known as the Miño Valley, a fertile landscape of hidden monasteries, stone farmhouses and vineyards.

Ribeiro white wines are produced in the Miño Valley, and for centuries the epicentre of production has been the beautifully preserved town of **Ribadavia**. As well as its attractive stone arcades and town houses, Ribadavia is famous throughout Spain for having maintained a sizeable Sephardic community, numbering half the town's population by the 14th century. In the old Jewish quarter, Hebrew inscriptions can be seen on the ancient walls. Slightly further southwest in **Melón**, the remains of the Mosteiro de Santa María del Melón is an evocative place, with mossy patches seeping through with the Romanesque renderings of the 12th-century structure.

Ourense is a buzzing and prosperous provincial capital. Head straight to the pedestrianised Cidade Vella (Old Centre) and the striking Praza Maior, flanked with fine examples of 19th-century town houses and their vernacular *galerías* (Number 4 is an art exhibition space run by the local bank). The splendid **Catedral de San Martíño** (*Rúa Coronel Ceano 1*) has preserved some original polychrome decoration on its Pórtico do Paraíso and has a lavish Renaissance chapel and choir.

To the northwest of Ourense, the Sil Valley is another wine-producing region, named after the Sil river, an estuary of the mighty Miño. It's a good place for walking, with thick forests of chestnut and oak and dramatic natural terraces, often blanketed in vines. Its most spectacular feature is the **Gargantas do Sil**, where the river cuts through rocky mountain walls over 300m (980ft) high.

Of the handful of monasteries that exist (or existed) in the valley (it was the monks who introduced the locals to winemaking), the nearby **Mosteiro**

GALICIAN CERAMICS

You'll find distinctive cobalt-blue and white ceramicware all over Galicia, in bars, restaurants and touted in the shops. The most famous maker of these lovely items is Sargadelos, a firm deeply entwined in the region's history and cultural renaissance. In 1804 high-quality kaolinite – the principal material in porcelain production – was found near the village of Sargadelos in northern Galicia. A factory was founded and flourished, but when the Napoleonic Wars broke out, the owners flew to Argentina and the factory was disbanded.

Flash forward to the end of the Spanish Civil War, when a group of Galician intellectuals got together to revive their native culture, which had suffered so badly under the iron fist of General Franco. From these meetings, the ovens of Sargadelos were fired up once more. The designs have changed little since then, with many figurines depicting local folkloric and political characters.

Santo Estero de Ribas del Sil is the most dramatic. After you wind up the mountain road above the gorge, its terracotta-red roofs and Gothic bell towers pop up over the ancient treetops like a scene from a fairy tale. Dating from the 10th–11th centuries, it has been heavily renovated for its new life as a *parador* (*see p149*), though the building is open to the general public (*Tel: 988 01 01 10*).

Rías Altas

North of Ferrol, the coast that arches all the way around to Asturias is known as the Rías Altas ('High Rivers'). In contrast to the Rías Baixas (*see opposite*), this coast is untamed and rugged, and the chilly waters keep tourist development at bay. Adventurers will find isolated villages situated in natural harbours, some fine stretches of beach and a constantly churning sea.

Spectacularly situated at the mouth of the Eo river, **Ribadeo**'s picture-perfect port is flanked with fine, colourful old town houses which once belonged to the town's prosperous sea merchants. Climb the steep cobblestoned streets to the centre of the town. Seek out the whimsical Casa dos Moreno in the Praza de España, a sterling example of belle-époque architecture with a distinctive look-out (window-enclosed tower). The statue of the dapper blue-coated gentleman is the Marqués de Sargadelos, founder of the famous Sargadelos ceramicmakers (*see box p35*). To the east, As Catedrals beach is one of the best around, named after the rock formations on the sand that recall Gothic arches.

As Catedrals beach near Ribadeo

A sandbar on Illas Cíes, on the Rías Baixas

Further west, **Viveiro** is another little gem. Enter the Cidade Vella (Old Centre) via the 16th-century Porta de Carlos V, a Renaissance gateway inspired by the Arc de Triomphe. Appropriately, the heart of the medieval city is the Igrexa de Santa María do Campo, a Romanesque church with a replica of the Lourdes grotto. Afterwards, walk through the Noriega Varela gardens to Covas, a 2km-long (1¼-mile) beach backed by a splendid Paseo Marítimo.

Rías Baixas

The southern stretch of the west coast, all the way down to Vigo, is known as the Rías Baixas ('Low Rivers'). While not as ruggedly beautiful as the Costa da Morte, and certainly more developed, populated and geared towards tourism, it has some beautiful, peaceful spots around the inlets and estuaries of the rivers and handful of islands. For foodies there are more mussels here than Brussels (they are cultivated in the rivers), and Galicia's most revered wine – the crisp, white Albariño – comes from the region.

Named after the biblical figure (who legend says anchored his ark on a nearby mount), **Noia** has a pair of Romanesque churches (Igrexa de San Martino and Igrexa de Santa María) and some fine beaches just further south (seek out **Oranda** near the hamlet of Portosín). The tiny hamlet of **Baroña**, just south of Porto do Son, has one of the best examples of *castros* (Celtic settlement remains) in Galicia – a cluster of circular foundations on a finger jutting out into the sea.

Other villages worth lingering in include **Padrón**, birthplace of Rosalía de Castro and Camilo José Cela, two literary giants (both have museums dedicated to their lives in the village), and **Cambados**, the hub of Galicia's Albariño country. Here, several *bodegas* can be visited (enquire at the tourist office), and you can learn about the area's wine production at the **Museo Etnográfico e do Viño** (*Avenida de Pastora 104. Open: Tue–Sun 10.30am–2pm & 4.30–7.30pm. Admission charge*).

Connected to the mainland by a bridge, the tiny island of **A Toxa** (La Toja in Castilian) is a household name in Spain. Mineral salts for A Toxa's famous soaps have been extracted from the island's waters for more than a century. Today, people flock to the elegant belle-époque hotel – mostly just to gawk at it – and to the nouveau-

GALICIAN FISHERMEN

Spain's demand for fish is insatiable, only trumped by that of the Japanese. Galicia's fishing fleet is the biggest in Europe and Spain's biggest supplier, but overfishing, coupled with the disastrous oil spill from the tanker *Prestige* in 2002, has rapidly depleted stocks, thus threatening the livelihood of this centuries-old culture. Lira, a tiny village on the Costa da Morte (*see pp30–31*), has taken the revolutionary steps of actually lowering their own quotas, creating a marine reserve and devising a direct sales network in order to make their industry more sustainable. Lira's *cofradía* (fishermen's guild) also offers day trips on a working fishing vessel, giving insight into their incredibly arduous craft (*see www.mardelira.net*).

riche villas dotted rather too heavily among the thick pine forests.

The area around **O Grove** on the mainland is more family-oriented, with large picnic areas, fine beaches (seek out **O Carreiro** on the opposite side of

The bridge to A Toxa

Basílica de Santa María, Pontevedra

the headland), windsurfing and kite-surfing facilities and pleasure boats for hire.

Pontevedra is the sort of town you may plan to spend an afternoon in but end up lingering a day or two. Roman in origin, its fine, remarkably intact Cidade Vella (Old Centre) is replete with splendid medieval buildings and churches (the Basílica de Santa María, situated on the town's highest point, has a richly rendered Plateresque façade), and at certain times of the day it seems as if time has stood still in this proud Galician town on the Lérez river. The renowned **Museo de Pontevedra** is located over several buildings including an old Jesuit college and a pair of fanciful Baroque mansions. This fascinating collection spans from Roman and Greek artefacts and coins to Celtic jewellery, painting and the

decorative arts, and includes a lovely collection of local Galician ceramic work. Not to be missed is the naval collection, which contains a re-creation of the 19th-century office of a local admiral (*Rúa Pasantería 2–12. Tel: 986 85 14 55. Open: Oct–May Tue–Sat 10am–2pm & 4–7pm, Sun 11am–2pm; Jun–Sept Tue–Sat 10am–2pm & 4.30–8.30pm, Sun 11am–2pm. Free admission for EU members*).

The three tiny islands (two are connected by a sandbank) that make up the archipelago of **Illas Cíes** are a must-visit for nature lovers, though it will take some effort. Declared a natural reserve in 1980, there is no accommodation on the islands apart from a camping ground (*see p151*), and they can only be reached via boat from Vigo, Baiona or Cangas during Easter week and summer (*Tel: 986 22 52 72*).

The waterfront in Vigo

The islands are renowned as a nesting ground for tens of thousands of waterfowl, most notably the yellowfoot seagull. Add to this the ruins of an old Celtic monastery, blankets of pine and eucalyptus forests, seductive coves and virgin beaches (Rodas Beach was recently named one of the Ten Best in the World by a British newspaper), and you will see why the Romans declared the Cíes the 'Islands of the Gods'.

Gritty, working-class but ultimately enjoyable, **Vigo** is Galicia's largest city. While its glory days as an important steamer ship hub have long passed, it still retains an air of graciousness, particularly around the cobblestoned old quarter near the port. These days it's mainly industrial fishing boats that pull up and anchor in Vigo, providing the city with a constant and plentiful supply of the fruits of the ocean. The

best place to try these is Berbés, the old fishermen's quarter of arcades and warehouses, filled with nicotine-stained bars serving up bubbling cauldrons of *pulbo* (octopus) and other tangled, shiny sea creatures. If that's a tad too authentic, head to the more tourist-friendly Praza de Piedra, where open-air cafés shuck oysters on the spot – the quintessential Vigoenese experience. For a seagull's eye view of Vigo, head to the Monte do Castro (a short walk from Berbés), a park with the remains of a castle. Part of its wall serves as a *mirador* for the bay of Vigo. You'll need to catch a bus (€1.15 from the centre) or a taxi to the impressive new **Museo do Mar**, set in a Modernist building (ingeniously converted from an old fish cannery) overlooking the bay. It has state-of-the-art exhibits on Galicia's maritime culture, ecosystems and

fishing industry, plus a small aquarium (*Avenida Atlántida 160.*
Tel: 986 24 77 50. Open: Jun–Sept Tue–Thur 10am–2pm & 5–10pm, Fri & Sat 10am–2pm & 4–10.30pm, Sun 10am–10pm; Oct–May Tue–Thur 10am–2pm & 4–8pm, Fri & Sat 10am–10.30pm, Sun 10am–9pm. Admission charge).

Santiago de Compostela

The simply enchanting city of Santiago de Compostela, capital of Galicia, is undoubtedly the region's trump card. Tens of thousands of pilgrims arrive here every year (*see 'Camino a Santiago', pp32–3*) and make their way directly to the colossal cathedral, where the whole history of the city is etched in stone. Though there are many magical places of interest in Santiago (*see 'Walk', pp42–3*), if your time is limited, make this sight the top of your list.

Make your way to Praza do Obradoiro, the cathedral's gateway. At 74m (242ft) high, its twin Baroque towers (added in the 18th century) soar over the old city skyline. Equally as humbling (and for many, the cathedral's most outstanding feature) are its various *portas* (doorways), most dating from the 11th–12th centuries and featuring exquisite carvings, the most mesmerising being the Pórtico da Gloria at the main entrance.

The Romanesque period dominates in the interior, with its signature austerity of barrel vaults, massive single nave, wide transept, fat pillars, and side bays and galleries. The high altar, in contrast, is a riot of Baroque ornamentation featuring the standard *cherubim* and other fancies of 18th-century flight. Behind the altar, visitors can access the supposed tomb of St James in the crypt, the original 9th-century foundations of the cathedral.

The cathedral's museum has a renowned tapestry collection and, when it's not swinging through the transept billowing out clouds of incense, a mammoth silver *botafumeiro*.
Cathedral. Tel: 981 58 35 48. Open: 7am–9pm; pilgrim mass daily at noon. Museum. Tel: 981 56 15 27. Open: Oct–May Mon–Sat 10am–1.30pm & 4–6.30pm; Jun–Sept 10am–2pm & 4–8pm. Admission charge.

Santiago's cathedral

Walk: Around Santiago de Compostela

This route will take you to most of the main sites within Santiago de Compostela's compact historic centre. The walk alone should take about an hour. Only a short distance is covered (approximately 2km/1¼ miles), but you need to take your time in order to really enjoy this mesmerising 'symphony in stone'. To get the full benefit, choose an hour that will coincide with a mass at the cathedral, and allow at least two hours if you plan to visit any of the museums mentioned.

Start your walk in the awe-inspiring Praza do Obradoiro, the epicentre of ancient Santiago de Compostela that marks the end of the pilgrims' journey.

1 La Catedral

Undoubtedly Santiago's biggest attraction and monument to St James,

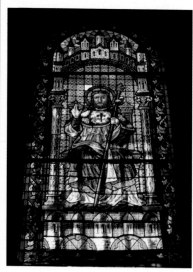

Stained glass in the cathedral

its two Baroque towers soar over the city's skyline. Your eyes will probably be diverted, however, to the mesmerising Pórtico da Gloria, a much-copied Romanesque work featuring magnificent sculptures of the prophets – the work of the sculptor Maestro Mateo. Seek out the kneeling figure of the Santo Dos Corques in the central column. Since time immemorial, Santiago's university students have believed that touching it will bring wisdom and good luck.

Turn around and walk to the opposite side of the Praza do Obradoiro.

2 Pazo de Raxoi (Raxoi Palace)

In contrast to the heady Gothic and Romanesque richness of the cathedral, the Pazo de Raxoi is the city's most important neoclassical building. Originally built in the 18th century to accommodate students, it has served as the city's seat of local government since 1970. Standing back from the monolithic, restrained façade, you can see a statue of St James on the roof.

Walk to the northern flank of the Praza do Obradoiro.

3 Hostal dos Reis Católicos

This edifice was commissioned by the Catholic monarchs Ferdinand and Isabella in 1492 as a hospital for pilgrims, who often arrived infirm. It later became a hostel. Added to over the centuries, it features various styles from Plateresque (or 'Silversmith's style') to Baroque and Late Gothic. Although it's now the city's most exclusive hotel (*see p171*), you are free to wander through the tranquil interior courtyards as a non-guest. Or better still, have a drink in the terrace café, which affords pretty vistas of the city's verdant surroundings.

Turn to your left and cross the Rúa de San Francisco.

4 Pazo de Xelmírez (Xelmírez Palace)

An important non-secular Romanesque work, this austere-looking building, adjacent to the northern part of the cathedral, was built in 1120 as a palace for the archbishop. It is now open to the public, and it's worth wandering around its rooms and stairways, some of which feature original relief work and columns (*same opening hours as the cathedral, see p41*).

Continue north along the Rúa de San Francisco to the end. Veer right, into the Rúa dos Castiñeiros.

Walk: Around Santiago de Compostela

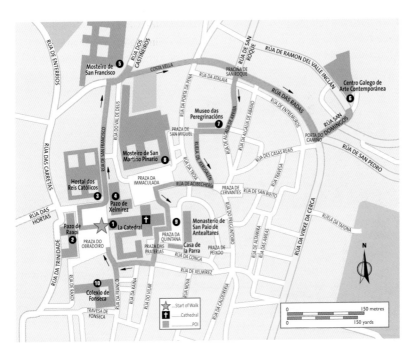

5 Mosteiro de San Francisco

The founding of this monastery (now a hotel) is ascribed to Francis of Assisi, who visited the city in the early 13th century. Not much remains of the original structure, though the 18th-century Baroque façade and bell towers make a nice contrast to the heavy medieval architecture of the Praza do Obradoiro.

Turn right, into the Costa Vella, cross the Praciña de San Roque square and continue along the Rúa das Radas, past the Porta do Camiño, to the end. Turn left into the Rúa San Domingos.

6 Centro Galego de Arte Contemporánea (Contemporary Arts Centre of Galicia)

For something completely different, the arts centre is one of the city's few Modernist buildings of note. The work of Portuguese architect Álvaro Siza Vieira (he also designed the Communications Campus at the city's university), it houses collections focusing on Galician artists from the 1960s onward (*Open: Tue–Sun 11am–8pm. Admission charge*).

Retrace your steps to the Praciña de San Roque. Turn left into the Rúa de Algalia de Arriba and then right, into the Praza de San Miguel.

7 Museo das Peregrinacións (Pilgrimage Museum)

Located inside a building known simply as the 'Gothic House' (though there are additions from the 17th century onwards), this small museum is dedicated to the pilgrims who come to Santiago, enlightening visitors through artefacts, paintings and ancient maps (*Open: Tue–Fri 10am–8pm, Sat*

Imposing architecture in the Praza do Obradoiro

10.30am–1.30pm & 5–8pm, Sun 10.30am–1.30pm. Admission charge). Exit the Praza de San Miguel south onto the Ruela de Xerusalén. Turn left into the Rúa de Acibechería and proceed to the Praza da Immaculada.

8 Mosteiro de San Martiño Pinario

Larger than the city's cathedral, this enormous Benedictine monastery, built between the 16th and 18th centuries, encloses no less than three sets of cloisters and a superb church with a dazzling Baroque façade and interior, the latter a work of Bartolomé Fernández Lechuga, a master of the movement. It is reached by a separate stairway, itself a work of art, on Praza de San Martiño, at the rear of the monastery (*Open: Tue–Sat 10.30am–2pm & 4–8.30pm. Admission charge). Exit south from the Praza da Immaculada and walk past the rear façade of the cathedral.*

Mosteiro de San Martiño Pinario

9 Praza da Quintana

This gem of a square, built over an old cemetery, was curiously designed over two levels connected by stairs, lending the space a theatrical feel, as if the upper plateau were a stage – and outdoor concerts are indeed often held here. Its focal point is a Baroque clock tower (known as the Berenguela) and the façade of the Casa da Parra, a handsome 17th-century building decorated with sculptures of plants and fruit on the frontage. Opposite is the façade of the Mosteiro de San Paio de Antealtares, which belongs to the oldest religious order in the city. It's well worth lingering in the Praza da Quintana at one of the handful of outdoor cafés.

Continue walking around the rear of the cathedral, then through the Praza das Praterías to the intersection of Rúa da Franco.

10 Colexio de Fonseca (Fonseca College)

This elegant 16th-century Renaissance edifice was built as part of the old university complex and today houses a library. Its highlights are the cloister, which bears a statue of Alonso Fonseca y Ulloa (an academic and once the archbishop of Santiago and later Toledo), and the main portal, which is richly decorated with figures of the saints.

Continue along the Rúa da Franco to the Praza do Obradoiro, your starting point.

Asturias and Cantabria

Asturias and neighbouring Cantabria are green, remote and mountainous. These are the very heartlands of Spain, home to some of its earliest human inhabitants and, later, the crucible of the Christian Reconquista (Reconquest) of the Iberian Peninsula. The spellbinding Picos de Europa attract most visitors, drawn by the abundant wildlife and pristine landscapes. But this region also boasts a stunning coastline, the Costa Verde, with a string of historic harbour towns that have become lovely, low-key resorts.

Art buffs will marvel at the exquisite pre-Romanesque churches and spectacular Paleolithic art, among the finest in Europe. By the end of the 8th century, Asturias was enjoying an extraordinary flowering in the arts, particularly architecture. While most of the rest of Europe was still lost in the Dark Ages, Asturian craftsmen and artists were creating their masterpieces: sublime churches built of stone instead of wood, decorated with lavish golden murals and adorned with splendid sculptures and metalwork. Cantabria enjoyed its artistic Golden Age even earlier – up to 16,000 years ago, when the enthralling depictions of running bison were first painted onto the walls of the Cave of Altamira.

Enthusiasts of outdoor sports and activities will find themselves spoilt for choice, with everything from superb hiking and mountain adventure sports to sailing and surfing. Foodies will enjoy the outstanding cheeses, seafood and cider; this region provides most of the dairy produce for all Spain, and the fish plucked from the Bay of Biscay is always superbly fresh.

ASTURIAS
Avilés

Ignore the scruffy industrial outskirts of Avilés and make straight for its delightful Casco Antiguo (Old Centre). Much of it dates from the 14th and 15th centuries, and its sinuous streets are lined with porticos and town houses, the latter painted in shades of pink and ochre. Tables spill out across the graceful squares, of which the grandest is the Plaza de España, known locally as the Plaza Mayor. Others include the arcaded Plaza de Abastos, where a weekly market takes place on Mondays. The leafy Parque de Ferrera, with its shady paths and duck pond, once belonged to the Marqués de Ferrera but is now a romantic public park. Avilés sits on the banks of the wide river of the same name, and is still one of the largest seaports in Asturias.

The piquant old fishermen's quarter of Sabugo makes for an enjoyable wander, particularly around the delightful square of Plaza del Carbayo. The Centro Niemeyer, a vast and gleaming-white international cultural centre, is under construction on the banks of the river. Designed by the prestigious Brazilian architect, it is his gift to the city and is due to open in 2010. The local beaches are justly famous, particularly the long, golden strands at Avilés' seaside satellite, Salinas, and the wilder beaches of the nearby headland of Cabo de Peñas.

Bárzana and Bermiego

Bárzana is the capital of the *comarca* (region) of Quirós, a quiet, rural mountain enclave about 20km (12 miles) south of Oviedo. The region is dotted with traditional villages, most of which still boast traditional Asturian houses built of stone with wooden balconies. In the last few years, tourism has joined farming and cattle-rearing as the main source of revenue for this region, and many of the old farmhouses have been converted into *casas rurales* (rural guesthouses, *see p150*). Much of the area is protected, and home to all kinds of wildlife, including the Cantabrian Brown Bear (*see box p59*), wolves, otters and eagles. There are several excellent hiking trails in these parts, including La Senda del Oso ('The Path of the Bear'), and fishing is also a popular activity. The little village of Bermiego contains two

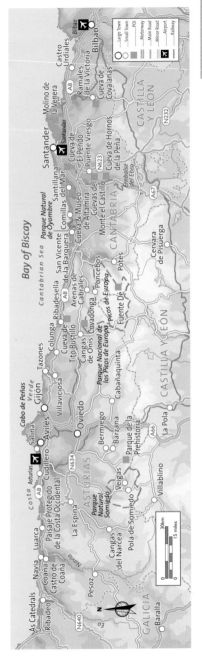

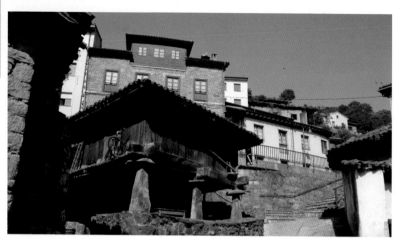

Traditional buildings in Bárzana

of the largest and oldest trees in Asturias: a 12m-high (39ft) oak, and a 7m-high (23ft) yew.

Castro de Coaña

More than 250 *castros* (ancient fortified settlements built by Celtic tribes some time before the arrival of the Romans) have been discovered in Asturias. The best preserved of these occupies a green hillside near the little town of Coaña, south of Navia, and contains the remnants of more than 80 circular dwellings. It's a magical spot, and enjoys lovely views over the valley. Slate, then as now, was a common building material in Asturias, and wild flowers peep between the dark-grey stones. It is thought that the earliest part of the settlement may date from the end of the Bronze Age in the 9th century BC, and that it accommodated between 1,500 and 2,000 people. The *castro* was

divided into two areas: the most important was the Acropolis, where cult rituals would have taken place; the other was largely residential, with a network of paths linking the buildings.

A small museum at the site offers a brief introduction to *castro* culture, about which very little is known. The huge granite stone at the entrance to the town of Coaña came from the *castro* and is known locally as the Estela Discoidea. It's covered on one side with faintly discernible markings that may have had some ancient ritual significance, perhaps relating to the sun or the moon. However, the stone was later Christianised and is now known as the Piedra de Nuestra Señora ('Stone of Our Lady').

Carretera AS12, Coaña. Tel: 985 97 84 01. Open: Apr–Sept Tue–Fri 11am–2pm & 4–7pm; Oct–Mar Tue–Sun 10am– 3pm. Closed: Mon. Free admission.

Cudillero

Lovely Cudillero is piled steeply around a narrow harbour. Its pretty houses, with their red-tiled roofs, are painted in pastel colours and cascade down the cliffside to the port. Farming and tourism may have become the town's biggest industries in recent years, but fishing and the sea are still at the very heart of Cudillero's identity. The fishing fleet, reduced but still substantial, returns to harbour every day between 5pm and 8pm, when you can watch the day's catch being unloaded onto the quays. Much of it will end up in the town's delightful *tascas* (bistros). The local patron saint, San Pedro, is venerated annually with an unusual celebration called the Amuravela, in which a sailor stands on a boat in the middle of the port and recites a witty sermon in the local dialect, *pixueto*. From the port, a path leads up to Cudillero's lighthouse, which enjoys spectacular views of the rugged coastline, and another path, called La Ruta de las Miradores, zigzags up through the steep village, stopping at panoramic viewing points (*miradores*) on the way. The coastline between Cudillero and Luarca, 40km (25 miles) west, is protected, and has some beautiful wild beaches and coves.

Gijón

The largest city in Asturias, Gijón is a big, busy seaport set amid industrial sprawl. But, although the modern outskirts have little to entice the visitor, its ancient heart is cheerful and decidedly attractive, with a pretty old fishermen's quarter piled up on a promontory (*see below*), a glossy marina with bobbing yachts, and a pair of long, sandy beaches.

Cimadevilla and around

The rocky promontory called Cimadevilla (literally 'top of the town') is now Gijón's liveliest and most alluring neighbourhood, a neatly-kept warren of narrow streets lined with old fishermen's cottages. At the very summit of the hill, where there are tremendous views, you'll find Eduardo Chillida's 1989 sculpture, *Elogio del Horizonte* ('Tribute to the Horizon'), which has become the city's symbol. The Cimadevilla is now packed with traditional bars and *tascas*, and is especially lively at weekends. More popular bars spread out their tables onto

Coastline west of Cudillero

Asturias and Cantabria

A café in the arcades of Plaza Mayor, Gijón

the grand, arcaded main square, the Plaza Mayor. Nearby, a beautiful 16th-century mansion – the birthplace of the Spanish Enlightenment statesman and writer Gaspar Jovellanos (1744–1811) – has been converted into a museum, the **Museo de Jovellanos** (*Plaza Jovellanos. Tel: 985 185 152. Open: Tue–Sat 9.30am–2pm & 5–7.30pm, Sun 10–2pm & 5–7.30pm. Free admission*). The **Museo Barjola** (*Calle Trinidad 13. Tel: 985 35 79 39. Open: Tue–Sat 11.30am–1.30pm & 5–8pm, Sun noon–4pm. Free admission*) offers an overview of the work of another of Gijón's famous sons, the painter Juan Barjola (1919–2004). East of the Plaza Mayor are the sparse remnants of the Baños Romanos (Roman Baths), virtually all that survives of the Roman settlement that was established here in the 1st century BC. Overlooking the marina on the western side of the promontory is the

Palacio de Revillagigedo, built in the 18th century over the ruins of a medieval tower. It is now a cultural centre and stages contemporary art exhibitions.

Other sights

Modern Gijón's greatest attractions are a pair of superb, sandy beaches: the Playa de Poniente to the east, and the Playa de San Lorenzo to the west. The city's modern **aquarium** (Acuario de Gijón) overlooks the Playa de Poniente, and its sharks, penguins, dolphins and sea turtles will keep kids amused for hours (*Tel: 985 18 52 20. Open: early Sept–Mar Mon–Fri 10am–7pm, Sat & Sun 10am–8pm; Easter week 10am–9pm; Apr–Jun Mon–Fri 10am–7pm, Sat & Sun 10am–9pm; Jul–Aug daily 10am–10pm; 1–8 Sept 10am–9pm. Admission charge*). On the outskirts of town, the **Museo del Pueblo de**

Asturias is an open-air ethnographic park that displays reconstructions of typical Asturian rural architecture, and also contains a museum dedicated to the *gaita*, or local bagpipes (*Paseo del Doctor Fleming 877. Tel: 985 18 29 60. Open: Sept–Jun Tue–Sat 10am–1pm & 5–8pm, Sun 11am–2pm & 5–7pm; Jul–Aug Tue–Sat 11am–1.30pm & 5–9pm, Sun 11am–2pm & 5–8pm. Admission charge*).

Oviedo

Oviedo, the capital of the Principality of Asturias, may come as a surprise. Until only a few years ago, it was shabby and neglected, but after a determined restoration project Oviedo has shrugged off its grimy coat to emerge as a ravishing little city which thoroughly enchants visitors. Many of its finest monuments date from the 9th century, when Alfonso II of Asturias

Asturias and Cantabria

Oviedo

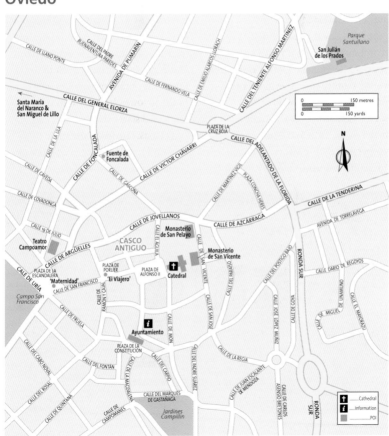

(791–842) established his court here and commissioned a series of glorious buildings. This was a golden age for Asturian pre-Romanesque architecture, which reached its apotheosis in a trio of remarkable churches.

Casco Antiguo (Old Centre)

Now that the grime has been scrubbed from the honey-coloured stone, the churches and mansions in Oviedo's historic centre gleam anew. The Plaza de Alfonso II is the city's oldest square, and Plaza de la Constitución is dominated by the splendid Ayuntamiento (Town Hall). Oviedo's spiritual heart is the Gothic **cathedral**, with a slender spire soaring above the rooftops. Although most of the present construction was built between the 14th and 16th centuries, it contains a 9th-century chamber specially commissioned by Alfonso II to house a much-venerated relic: a fragment of the Holy Shroud. This chamber (called the Cámara Santa) still displays the cathedral's most precious treasures, including the golden Crucifix reputed to have been carried by the Asturian leader Pelayo at Covadonga (*see p10*), and a cup said to be the Holy Grail. The Holy Shroud, however, is only brought out on special feast days. In the early years of the *Reconquista*, the presence of these relics underlined Oviedo's place as an important Christian city, and it attracted a stream of devout pilgrims from across Europe. Several Asturian and Leonese monarchs from the 8th to the 10th centuries are interred in the Royal Pantheon in the main basilica.

As part of Oviedo's dramatic restoration programme, a number of contemporary artworks were

Tiled façade in Oviedo's Casco Antiguo

commissioned for public spaces. Among the best loved are Eduardo Úrculo's *El Viajero* ('The Traveller') on the Plaza de Porlier, and Ferdinand Botero's *Maternidad* ('Maternity') on the Plaza de la Escandalera.

Pre-Romanesque architecture

The jewel in the crown of the city's extraordinary pre-Romanesque churches can be found a short walk from the cathedral. **San Julián de los Prados** (also known as Santullano), commissioned by Alfonso II, is the oldest and largest of the surviving Asturian churches, and contains some remarkably beautiful and well-preserved frescoes.

Two more exquisite churches sit on a hillside just north of the city, best reached by local bus. The grandest,

Santa María del Naranco, was built for King Ramiro I (*c.* 790–850) and functioned as a summer palace before being converted into a church. The smaller church of **San Miguel de Lillo**, substantially remodelled in the 18th century, was Ramiro I's royal chapel, and contains some vestiges of its original frescoes.

Parque Natural Somiedo (Somiedo Natural Park)

In the southeastern corner of Asturias, the natural park of Somiedo is a magnificent, mountainous, protected region which is home to a vast array of plant, bird and animal life. One of the last populations of the Cantabrian Brown Bear (*see box p59*) lives among these rugged peaks and dense forests, along with wolves, otters, capercaillie

Cows grazing in the east of the Parque Natural Somiedo

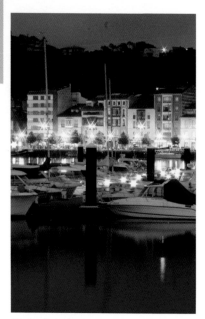

Ribadesella harbour

and golden eagles. A few traditional Asturian villages are scattered amid the wilderness, where some hardy locals still raise livestock according to time-honoured traditions. In the little village of Veigas, Somiedo's fascinating open-air **Ecomuseo** (*Tel: 985 76 39 84. www.somiedo.es. Open: Oct–Apr Tue–Sat 10am–2pm & 4–6pm, Sun 11am–2pm; May–Sept Tue–Sat 11am–2pm & 5–8pm, Sun 11am–2pm. Admission charge*) displays examples of the circular, stone-built thatched huts used by the few surviving cattle-drivers in summer. There are several spectacular hikes throughout the region, and you can find information at the park's **Centro de Interpretación** in Pola de Somiedo (*Tel: 985 76 37 58*).

Ribadesella

Straddling the Sella river just as it empties into the sea, the colourful seaside town of Ribadesella boasts an enchanting historic centre, a picture-postcard harbour packed with tapas bars and restaurants, a breathtaking mountain backdrop and a broad, sandy beach. If lazing about on the beach ever pales, there are all kinds of other activities to choose from, including canoeing on the river.

There are numerous caves in the vicinity, which have been inhabited since prehistoric times. Most famous is the **Cueva de Tito Bustillo**, which contains some superb paintings depicting animals (including some beautifully rendered horses) and fertility symbols. They were created between 25,000 and 12,000 BC and adorn a series of connected subterranean chambers (*Tel: 985 86 11 20. Open: end-Mar–mid-Sept Wed–Sun 10am–4.30pm. Closed: Mon & Tue. Admission charge & admission by guided visit in Spanish only*). The visit takes 60 minutes, children under 12 are not admitted, and the cave is not suitable for the infirm or anyone frightened of enclosed spaces. Pre-booking is advised.

Even earlier inhabitants of the region – dinosaurs – have left their mark in the form of footprints, found along the coast between Ribadesella and Villaviciosa. You can find out more at the child-friendly **Museo Jurásico de Asturias** (Jurassic Museum) in Colunga, a modern museum shaped like a dinosaur footprint, with lots of

ASTURIAN CIDER

Cider, an alcoholic drink made with pressed apples, is popular across Northern Spain, but *sidra asturiana* is considered the finest. Asturias is the only cider-producing region to have its own DOP (*Denominación de Origen Protegida*), which ensures that only locally-grown, indigenous apples are used in production. The traditional method of serving Asturian cider is to hold the bottle at head height (or above) and pour a small quantity into a wide-mouthed glass held at hip height. This 'aerates' the cider, and gives it small, Champagne-like bubbles.

interactive exhibits (*Tel: 902 30 66 00. Open: mid-Jun–mid-Sept daily 10.30am–2.30pm & 4–8pm; mid-Sept–mid-Jun Wed–Sun 10.30am–2.30pm & 4–7pm. Admission charge*).

Villaviciosa

Sitting pretty on the banks of the Río de Villaviciosa, the affluent town of the same name is famous throughout Spain for its delicious cider (*see box above*), which has been made here since the 19th century. Villaviciosa means 'fertile town', and in spring thousands of apple trees (known in local dialect as *pumaraes*) burst into bloom. It's a handsome place, scattered with the ornate mansions built by returning *Indianos* – the half-envious, half-disparaging name given to locals who had made their fortune in the Americas. Countless *sidrerías* (cider houses) offer the traditional Asturian tipple, accompanied by delicious local delicacies. Approximately 11km (7 miles) away, where the river opens

into the sea, is the little fishing port of Tazones, where Carlos I (who ruled the Holy Roman Empire as Charles V) first set foot in Spain in 1517. The event is enacted annually during the village's summer festival (held in mid-August).

CANTABRIA
Castro Urdiales

Castro Urdiales is a fine old harbour town in eastern Cantabria, near the border with the Basque Country. Once it was one of the most powerful towns on the northern coast, part of an influential confederation which guarded the region's interests against those of other European ports. Eventually, the town

(*Cont. on p58*)

Apple sculpture in Villaviciosa

Cantabrian cave art

Cantabria's wealth of Paleolithic archaeological sites is unequalled anywhere in the world. The most famous is the Cueva de Altamira, inhabited by Magdalenian hunter-gatherers between 16,000 and 9,000 BC. Altamira, along with 17 other decorated Cantabrian and Asturian caves, has been declared a World Heritage Site by UNESCO. The cavern is magnificently decorated with spellbinding paintings that exhibit such skill, delicacy and vivacity that they have been called the 'Sistine Chapel of Paleolithic art'. Most of the paintings depict animals, mainly bison (although horses and deer are also represented), that seem to gallop across the ceiling. The technical prowess is astonishing: the rocky outcrops of the cave surface have been cunningly incorporated into the artworks to heighten the illusion of movement; delicate shading adds nuance; and the fur and manes are drawn with a precise realism. The effect is breathtaking. Picasso was moved to proclaim: 'After Altamira, all is decadence.'

The Cueva de Altamira has now been closed to visitors in order to protect the irreplaceable paintings. An exact reproduction, called the Neocueva, has been built in the adjoining **Museo de Altamira**, which offers a fascinating introduction to the early human cultures that lived in this region many thousands of millennia ago (*Santillana del Mar. Tel: 942 81 88 15. http://museodealtamira.mcu.es. Open: May–Oct Tue–Sat 9.30am–8pm, Sun & public holidays 9.30am–3pm; Nov–Apr Tue–Sat 9.30am–6pm, Sun & public holidays 9.30am–3pm. Closed: Mon, 1 & 6 Jan, 1 May, 24, 25 & 31 Dec. Admission charge*).

To see authentic Paleolithic art in situ, visit the extensive and atmospheric **Cuevas del Monte el Castillo** in Puente Viesgo, south of Santander (*Tel: 942 59 84 25. Open: Nov–Feb Tue–Sun 9.30am–3pm; Mar–mid-Jun & mid-Sept–Oct Tue–Sun 9.30am–2.30pm & 3.30–6pm; mid-Jun–mid-Sept daily*

Bison painting at Altamira

The Museo de Altamira holds a reproduction of the Cueva de Altamira

9.30am–8pm. *Admission charge, &
admission by guided visit in Spanish
only*). There is something
extraordinarily thrilling about actually
being in the presence of Paleolithic
artworks in their original environment.
It's not hard to picture the early
humans painting by the light of a fire
or simple torches.

Other fascinating caves include the
Cueva de El Pendo in Escobedo de
Camarga, the Cueva de Covalanas in
Ramales de la Victoria, and the Cueva
de Hornos de la Peña.

The Cantabrian tourist board provides
comprehensive information on visiting
hours and facilities in all its cave sites, as
well as an online ticket booking service
at *http://cuevas.culturadecantabria.com*

The neighbouring region of
Asturias has its own share of
outstanding Paleolithic cave art, that

has also been recognised by
UNESCO. Foremost among the
treasures is the Cueva de Tito Bustillo
(*see 'Ribadesella', pp54–5*), that
contains some exquisitely rendered
animals, particularly horses.

Asturias has a modern museum
dedicated to prehistoric cave art called
the **Parque de la Prehistoria**, set in
unspoilt countryside 40km (25 miles)
south of Oviedo (*San Salvador de
Alesga, near Teverga. Tel: 902 30 66
00. www.parquedelaprehistoria.com.
Open: Dec–Feb Thur–Sun 10.30am–
5pm; Mar–mid-Jun & mid-Sept–Nov
Wed–Sun 10.30am–2.30pm &
4–7pm; mid-Jun–mid-Sept daily
10.30am–2.30pm & 4–8pm.
Admission charge*). Exhibits cover the
finest cave art in Europe, putting the
paintings of Asturias and Cantabria
into their European context.

lost its medieval prestige to other Spanish towns, but tourism has provided it with new sources of income in the last few decades. The pretty stone harbour and elegant old town are flanked on either side by gorgeous beaches overlooked by modern villa developments, and restaurant-lined seafront promenades. It's a happy marriage of old and new, which attracts thousands of visitors every year.

Castro Urdiales is still an important fishing port, and famous for the delectable anchovies prized by gourmets throughout the world. Colourfully painted wooden fishing boats are lined up along the stone wharfs of the lovely old port, which is overlooked by the splendid Gothic church of Santa María de la Asunción. Begun in the 12th century but only completed 400 years later, it bristles with buttresses and contains some fine artworks, including a painting attributed to Zurbarán. A

Castro Urdiales port

Roman milestone, found in the square in front of the church, and a pretty Roman bridge are witness to the town's ancient origins. Nearby, the shell of a medieval castle built by the Templar Knights has been transformed into a quirky lighthouse.

Comillas

Elegant Comillas has been a fashionable seaside resort since the end of the 19th century, when wealthy aristocrats commissioned the extravagant *Modernista* villas which still adorn the town. Finest among them is El Capricho, an early work by the visionary Catalan architect Antoni Gaudí, who created an elaborate neo-Mudéjar folly complete with fairy-tale towers in the 1880s. (The former villa is now a smart restaurant and also contains a shop selling Gaudí-themed souvenirs.) The Palacio de Sobrellano, a splendid neo-Gothic edifice commissioned by the first Marqués de Comillas in 1878, was designed by another leading Catalan architect, Joan Martorell. Most impressive of all is the Universidad Pontificia, designed by Lluís Domènech i Montaner (the architect responsible for the glorious Palau Música Catalana in Barcelona), a massive red-brick complex set in parkland which crowns a gentle hill. The university moved to Madrid and the building is now owned by the Cantabrian government, which is renovating it to house another academic institution.

El Capricho, designed by Antoni Gaudí, is now a restaurant in Comillas

Once you've taken in the *Modernista* highlights, Comillas, as befits an upmarket resort, offers fine dining and elegant shopping. The main beach is a beautiful stretch of fine white sand, but the undulating coastline offers plenty of smaller, quieter coves to explore.

San Vicente de la Barquera

Another traditional fishing port which has turned to tourism in recent years, San Vicente de la Barquera has maintained its salty, maritime character, particularly around the colourful port. It was fishing, after all, that made its fortune and ensured its wealth and influence for centuries. It still preserves numerous fine monuments, including a splendid Gothic church, the Iglesia de Santa María de los Ángeles, which contains the elaborate marble tomb of the *inquisitor* Antonio del Corro (1472–1556). A story-book castle, begun in 1210 on the ruins of an earlier

fortress, has been converted into a cultural centre, with art exhibitions and performances. And the beautiful, ivy-clad Convento de San Luís hosted Carlos I (also called Charles V, Holy Roman Emperor) in 1517, when he travelled to Spain for his coronation as King of Spain. Perhaps the town's most emblematic

CANTABRIAN BROWN BEAR (OSO PARDO CANTÁBRICO)

The Cantabrian Brown Bear (*Ursus arctos*), which once roamed freely through the mountains, is in danger of extinction in Spain. Hunting, although illegal and punished by massive fines, is largely responsible for the diminishing numbers. The bears have been reduced to just two isolated populations in southern Asturias: the eastern colony numbers 25 to 30 bears, and the western colony has around 100 bears. Conservation efforts are currently being concentrated on joining the two groups, which will genetically strengthen their chances of survival. To find out more, contact the Fundación Oso Pardo (*www.fundacionosopardo.org*).

monument is the Puente de la Maza, an elegant and incredibly long Baroque bridge that spans the broad river.

Much of the stunning coastline around San Vicente de la Barquera is part of the Parque Natural de Oyambre, a protected region of cliffs, dunes and rolling hills, which is both extraordinarily beautiful and blessedly unspoiled.

Santander

Santander, capital of Cantabria, has a split personality: it is both a busy modern seaport and an elegant summer resort, which first became fashionable during the mid-19th century.

Central Santander

There is little to see in Santander's old centre, which was destroyed by fire in 1941, although its lively bars and restaurants give it plenty of buzz on summer evenings, particularly around the waterfront. The cathedral, begun in the 12th century but incinerated in 1941, has been rebuilt, and is notable for its cool, stone cloister, and a gruesome reliquary containing the heads of two early Roman martyrs. Nearby, the exuberant market, El Mercado de la Esperanza, is a great place to pick up picnic supplies or choose gourmet treats to take home.

There is a clutch of interesting museums, including the **Museo Marítimo** (Maritime Museum), with exhibits relating to Santander's long seafaring tradition, and a giant whale skeleton (*Calle San Martín de Bajamar. Tel: 942 27 49 62. Open May–Sept daily 10am–7.30pm, last admission 6.30pm; Oct–April daily 10am–6pm, last admission 5pm. Admission charge*). The **Museo de Prehistoria y Arqueología** (Museum of Prehistory and Archeology, *temporarily closed – check with the tourist office for details*) offers a good introduction to Cantabria's fascinating early history and its prehistoric cave art.

A stretch of beach at El Sardinero

Santa Juliana's remains are kept in the Colegiata

El Sardinero

The seaside suburb of El Sardinero, with its belle-époque mansions and lavish casino, was spared in a terrible fire in 1941. This affluent neighbourhood overlooks two of the finest city beaches (La Primera and La Segunda). There are more splendid strands on either side of the Peninsula de la Magdalena, which divides El Sardinero from the workaday city centre. The peninsula is crowned by a fairy-tale palace, originally built in the first years of the 20th century as a gift to King Alfonso XIII, and now part of Santander's prestigious summer university.

Santillana del Mar

Often described as the prettiest village in Spain, Santillana del Mar is beautifully set amid woodland and rolling hills 4km (2¹/₂ miles) from the coast. According to an old local saying, Santillana is neither saintly (santo), nor flat (llana), nor by the sea (del Mar): 'Santillana no es santa, no es llana, y no hay mar'. Its name actually derives from Santa Juliana (also known as Santa Illana), a 3rd-century AD martyr whose relics are still kept in the Colegiata (Collegiate Church), a Benedictine monastery first erected in the 12th century (although later substantially remodelled). In the 14th century, local nobles began to build lavish residences, adorning them with huge coat of arms. These splendid palaces survive perfectly preserved in the cobbled streets of Santillana's enchanting old town. Despite its picture-postcard charm and the constant hordes of day trippers, Santillana del Mar has somehow managed to avoid becoming a museum town, and is an authentic and down-to-earth little community which is a delight to explore. Spend the night if you can, to enjoy it without the crowds. It is just 2km (just over a mile) from the Cueva de Altamira, which contains some of the earliest and most extraordinary paintings in the world (*see p56*).

Picos de Europa

The mighty Picos de Europa mountain range straddles three Spanish regions: Asturias, Cantabria and Castilla y León. The area covers around 650sq km (250sq miles) and much of it is now protected as a national park – the largest in Europe. Within its boundaries are some of the most spectacular landscapes on the Iberian Peninsula, with craggy peaks (some of which remain snow-capped year-round), glacial lakes, meadows flecked with wild flowers, and lush valleys. The range begins just 20km (12½ miles) from the northern coast, and may have acquired its name – which means 'Peaks of Europe' – from sailors, for whom the jagged terrain may have been their first sight of home after months or even years at sea.

The park is a very popular destination for hikers and mountain climbers, with several excellent walking trails suitable for visitors of all fitness levels and abilities, and some challenging peaks for rock climbers. Other activities include canyoning, pot-holing, whitewater rafting, horse riding and canoeing.

Cangas de Onís is the main access town for the Picos, while medieval Potes, to the east, is perhaps the prettiest and has become a major centre for adventure tourism. Both offer a good range of accommodation and other services. Arenas de Cabrales is known throughout Spain for its pungent cheese, which is traditionally left to mature in a cave. Thickly veined with blue and eye-wateringly strong, it's served in almost every local restaurant, and is available in countless local shops. Cabrales cheese is perhaps the best known of the delicacies from the Picos de Europa, but you'll find wonderful honey, cured meats and artisan cheeses throughout the region.

Puenta la Vidre in the Picos de Europa

Cable car at Fuente Dé

On the northwest border of the park is Covadonga, a celebrated cave-shrine beautifully set above a rushing waterfall. This shrine and its much venerated image of the Madonna are a hugely popular pilgrimage spot, with a very important place in Asturian culture. According to tradition, the Madonna appeared to Pelayo, the Visigothic noble who founded the Kingdom of Asturias, who was hiding out in this cave with his small band of supporters. She ensured his victory in the decisive battle against the Moors which took place here around 722 – the first important defeat against the Muslim armies. Pelayo and his wife are buried in the shrine.

The park can get crowded, particularly in July and August. The roads can get unpleasantly clogged, and access to some areas, particularly the Covadonga lakes, is restricted to a fixed number of visitors, so arrive early if you are determined to visit. The **Fuente Dé** cable car is another popular tourist attraction (*near Liebana. Tel: 942 73 66 10. Open: winter 10am–6pm; summer 9am–8pm. Admission charge*). It soars up for almost 2,000m (6,500ft) to a spectacular viewing point (*mirador*) and the start of some fantastic walking trails. Queues are likely in summer, but the stunning panorama may make up for the wait.

Maps and information are available from **park information offices** in Cangas de Onís (*Avenida Covadonga 43. Tel: 985 84 86 14*), Posada de Valdeón (*El Ferial. Tel: 987 74 05 49*), Cillórigo de Liébana (*Avenida Luis Cuevas 2-A, Tama. Tel: 942 73 05 55*), and from **tourist information offices** in popular destinations such as Potes (*Tel: 942 73 07 87*) and Arenas de Cabrales (*Tel: 985 84 64 84*).

Basque Country

The Basques are one of the oldest peoples in Europe, with a unique language and culture entirely different from those of surrounding territories. It is a breathtakingly beautiful region, with rolling hills of emerald green, a rugged coastline dotted with exquisite fishing villages, and a magnificent reputation for its cuisine. Bilbao's Guggenheim Museum has become one of the biggest visitor attractions in Europe, and the graceful belle-époque seaside resort of Donostia-San Sebastián hosts a glittering annual film festival.

The Basque Country has remained deliciously untouched, particularly in the remote inland regions. Here, villagers still celebrate their local festivals in the time-honoured way with feats of strength which have changed little in centuries. Basque is widely spoken, and traditional games like *pelota* can be seen everywhere. The fierce pride in Basque culture is ever present, evident in the monumental sculptures of Eduardo Chillida, and the spreading oak tree which served as the traditional assembly in the ancient Basque capital of Gernika-Lumo. And nowhere is Basque pride more evident than in its cuisine – both the traditional fare served up in atmospheric seafront taverns, and the innovative *cocina creativa* which has been garlanded with numerous awards in the region's top restaurants. The Basque gastronomic capital is undoubtedly Donostia-San Sebastián, where the celebrated tapas bars groan under the weight of extravagant platters of *pintxos* (tapas), justly described as 'miniature works of art'.

Bergara

Bergara (known in Castilian Spanish as Vergara) is a beautiful country town that has retained a handsome ensemble of 16th- and 17th-century palaces and churches in its mellow old centre. Finest among them is the church of San Pedro de Ariznoa, begun in the late 16th century and completed in 1742 when the solid bell tower was added. During the Carlist Wars, which split Spain for most of the 19th century, Bergara served as the Carlist base and court. It was here that the treaty was signed which ended the first Carlist War (1833–9). Bergara is surrounded by rolling green hills through which hiking trails meander between ancient dolmens and megalithic burial tombs.

Bilbao

Little more than a decade ago, few people had ever heard of Bilbao. A number of heavy industries were clustered here, as well as a major port. From the 1980s, with industry in decline, the city needed to rethink its image. It began an ambitious regeneration programme which saw the complete renovation of its infrastructure, and which had, as its centrepiece, a new outpost of the Guggenheim Museum. A dazzling design by Frank Gehry was chosen for the museum, which opened in 1997 to outstanding popular and critical acclaim. In the wake of the Guggenheim Effect (*see pp68–9*),

Bilbao has became a fashionable tourist destination, and the city has continued its bold reforms.

Casco Viejo (Old Centre)

Bilbao began here, on the banks of the Nervión river, in the 13th century. The Siete Calles ('Seven Streets') that make up the heart of the Old Centre still retain something of their old village feel. They are lined with traditional tapas bars and restaurants, and are

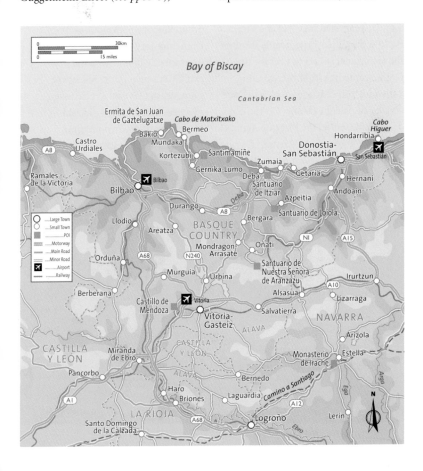

particularly lively at weekends. There's a wonderful little museum of Basque history, the **Museo Vasco**, which occupies a Baroque cloister (*Plaza Miguel de Unamuno 4. Tel: 944 15 54 23. www.euskal-museoa.org. Open: Tue–Sat 11am–5pm, Sun 11am–2pm. Closed: public holidays. Admission charge*). From the nearby square, a lift swoops up to the Begoña neighbourhood: it's worth it just for the incredible views, but locals come for the Basílica de Begoña, which contains a much-venerated image of the Virgin. Back in the Casco Viejo, amble through the traditional streets to find the little Gothic cathedral, built between the 14th and 16th centuries, with a delicate cloister of pale grey stone. On the edge of the Old Centre, the Plaza de Arriaga, popularly known as La Arenal, is overlooked by the lavish opera house, the Teatro Arriaga.

Guggenheim Museum

Nestled at the heart of the city, on the banks of the river which made Bilbao's fortune, Frank Gehry's glorious 'titanium flower' has been described as the world's finest building. As much sculpture as edifice, it is a vast, shimmering construction with billowing 'sails' that glisten as they catch the light. There is only one permanent exhibit: Richard Serra's magnificent *The Matter of Time*, a series of huge, sinuous, rusted iron pieces occupying one enormous gallery. Contemporary art features most prominently in the temporary exhibitions held in the rest of the museum but, as well as celebrated modern artists such as Takashi Murakami or Cy Twombly, the Guggenheim has exhibited everything from the fashion of Giorgio Armani to a selection of highlights from Vienna's

Crossing the river in Bilbao's old town

Kunsthistoriches Museum. In high season, it's worth booking tickets in advance. This is also true if you are hoping to dine in the Guggenheim restaurant, run by celebrity Basque chef Martín Berasategui.

Abandoibarra etorbidea 2. Tel: 944 35 90 00. www.guggenheim-bilbao.es. Open: Sept–Jun Tue–Sun 10am–8pm; Jul–Aug daily 10am–8pm. Admission charge.

Other sights

Bilbao's newly expanded **Museo de Bellas Artes** (Museum of Fine Arts) contains masterpieces by Zurbarán, El Greco and Goya (*Museo Plaza 2. Tel: 944 39 60 60. www.museobilbao.com. Open: Tue–Sun 10am–8pm. Admission charge*). You can learn more about the city's long seafaring tradition at the **Museo Marítimo Ría de Bilbao**, a striking modern museum filled with interactive exhibits (*Muelle Ramón de la Sota 1. Tel: 902 13 10 00. www. museomaritimobilbao.org. Open: Tue–Fri 10am–6.30pm, Sat & Sun 10am–8pm. Admission charge*). Some of the best of Bilbao's shops and restaurants are clustered in the 19th-century extension to the Old Centre, called El Ensanche. Football fans might want to make the pilgrimage to **Estadio de San Mamés** (*Calle Felipe Serrate*), the home stadium of Atlético Club de Bilbao.

Castillo de Mendoza

The Castillo de Mendoza has been much restored but retains its original medieval aspect: a single, solid tower-house sits in the centre and is surrounded by a fortified wall with a watchtower at each of the four corners. The main tower house has been converted into the **Museo Heráldica** (Museum of Heraldry), which contains some superb stone heraldic shields from the Álava region's ancestral homes, as well a general introduction to the art of heraldry (*Open: Tue–Fri 11am–2pm & 4–8pm, Sat 11am–3pm, Sun & public holidays 10am–2pm*).

Deba

Deba sits at the mouth of the wide Deba river, which opens out here into the sea. It has been a fashionable resort since the early 20th century, and its huge sandy beach is backed by a smattering of gorgeous belle-époque-style villas in ice-cream colours. There isn't much left of Deba's historic centre, but a few churches and palaces have survived the centuries, including the graceful 16th-century Gothic church of Santa María. In the hills behind the town is the Santuario de Itziar, a fortress-like sanctuary which dates from the 13th century and still attracts thousands of pilgrims annually. It contains a much-venerated Romanesque image of the Virgin, patron saint of sailors.

Deba is tucked between a fold in the hills, and boat trips depart daily from here in summer to admire the stunning cliffs. A magnificent cliff walk links Deba with the very popular seaside resort of Zumaia.

The Guggenheim Effect

Frank Gehry's breathtaking Guggenheim Museum, with its billowing swirls of titanium, opened in 1997. Suddenly, Bilbao – formerly a run-down industrial city that almost no one had heard of – was on the international map, attracting an astonishing deluge of visitors. The museum paid for itself within a year, and it is estimated that its current economic impact on the city is around €170 million annually. Lesser-known cities around the world began to daydream of commissioning a 'starchitect', one of the new generation of celebrity architects, to create a flagship building that would bring in huge crowds and massive investment. The 'Guggenheim Effect', also known as the 'Bilbao Effect', was born.

The museum was key to Bilbao's extraordinary rise in the fashion stakes, but it was only one part of a massive and ongoing regeneration plan that featured a starry array of internationally famous architects. A sleek new metro system, designed by Norman Foster, first opened in 1995 and is still being expanded. The entrances – huge, curved, glassy tubes which seem to erupt from the pavements – have become a city icon, and are affectionately called 'Fosteritos'. Santiago Calatrava created the shimmering white airport that looks like a great bird in flight, as well as a glassy bridge which crosses the Nervión river in the city centre, and Rafael Moneo designed the new University library.

The city's fine arts museum, the Museo de Bellas Artes, was expanded and remodelled, and is now one of the largest in Spain. A new, high-tech museum dedicated to Bilbao's maritime history was also built, the Museo Marítimo Bilbao, in a vast edifice which resembles the ships once constructed here. Nearby, the massive Palacio Euskalduna, an award-winning congress centre and concert hall designed by Federico Soriano and Dolores Palacios,

Calatrava's Zubizuri bridge

Frank Gehry's creation sits next to the Nervión

was inaugurated in 1999. The Nervión – once rank and polluted – has been dramatically cleaned up, and parks and cycling paths now line its banks. A bright green tram now snakes its way through the newly restored centre, cleaned of its graffiti and grime. Visitors can also enjoy a host of chic restaurants, shops and bars. Bilbao once offered bland business hotels and shabby *pensiones* and little else but, again thanks to the Guggenheim, sleek designer establishments have been mushrooming across the city, the Gran Domine, Hotel Miró and Hesperia Bilbao among them.

Current and future projects include the conversion of Bilbao's old municipal wine storage facility, the Alhóndiga, a lavish 19th-century building in the city's old centre. Philippe Starck is part of the team behind the project, which is transforming the facility into a stunning arts and entertainment centre. It is hoped that it will stage its first exhibition in 2010, although it won't be fully completed until 2012. Zaha Hadid has put forward an ambitious plan to entirely redevelop Bilbao's neglected Zorrozaurre peninsula, which she plans to turn into an island linked to the mainland with eight bridges. The newly formed island has a land area of 72 hectares (180 acres) and will accommodate about 6,000 homes and a new technology centre. The estimated cost of the project is a staggering €1.5 billion. Work is scheduled to begin in 2010 and be completed between 2025 and 2030.

Watching Bilbao reinvent itself has been an amazing experience for the last decade – and the city looks set to outdo itself over the next decade or so.

Donostia-San Sebastián

Donostia is a glorious Basque city, spread around a perfect curve of golden sand and overlooked by a pair of verdant capes. From 1885, the Queen Regent María Cristina brought the Spanish court here every summer, cementing its reputation as the country's most fashionable resort. Modern Donostia has an atmospheric Parte Vieja (Old Quarter), an elegant 19th-century extension with frothy belle-époque buildings, and an outstanding reputation for its cuisine.

Although the city is better known outside Spain by its Castilian Spanish name of San Sebastián, its official name is Donostia-San Sebastián, usually shortened simply to Donostia (or sometimes 'San Se') locally.

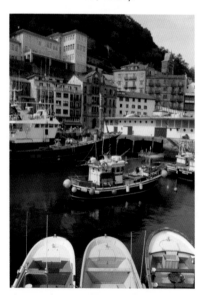

The port of Donostia-San Sebastián

Área Romántica (Romantic Quarter)

In 1863, the medieval walls which contained old Donostia were finally pulled down. An elegant new neighbourhood was erected and has become known as the Área Romántica. This neighbourhood now contains fashionable boutiques, restaurants and cafés, as well as the graceful neoclassical cathedral (erected in the 1880s) and the sumptuous Teatro Victoria Eugenia (completed in 1914), which hosts the International Film Festival.

Bahía de la Concha and the seafront

The beach of La Concha is a magnificent crescent-shaped strand backed with sumptuous belle-époque hotels and residences. It is fringed by an elegant promenade, which has been the city's favourite spot for the evening *paseo* (stroll) for more than a century. Sitting atop a rocky outcrop in the middle of the beach is the Palacio de Miramar, once the summer home of the Spanish royal family. West of the palace stretches the beach of Ondarreta, which culminates in the steep Monte Igueldo. Atop this headland is a funicular and a small funfair – a romantic spot at dusk, with beautiful views. At the base of the headland is a vast, 1976 boxy sculpture by Basque artist Eduardo Chillida (1924–2002) called *Peine del Viento XV* ('Comb of the Wind'). Out in the middle of the bay is the pretty little islet of Santa Clara, shaped just like a turtle. Boats take visitors out to spend the day picnicking on its delightful beaches in summer.

Parte Vieja (Old Quarter)

The oldest part of Donostia sits huddled at the foot of Monte Urgell, a green headland which shelters the little port. The Parte Vieja is a delightful, largely pedestrianised warren of narrow streets, dotted with churches and squares and crammed with outstanding tapas bars. The Plaza de la Constitución is a magnificent enclosed square, flanked on all sides with arcades. One of the few buildings to escape the terrible fire of 1813 is the church of Santa María del Coro, a florid Baroque church dedicated to the city's patron saint, an image of the Black Madonna. It plays a key part in Donostia's biggest traditional events, the Semana Grande in August, and the Tamborrada, which takes place on 20 January, the feast day

BASQUE SPORTS

Herri Kirolak, Basque rural sports, have been an important part of Basque village festivals for centuries. They usually require feats of great strength, and include stone-lifting, tug-of-war and raising an ox-cart. The winners are rewarded with a Basque beret (*txapela*). Pelota is the best-known Basque sport, and has been exported around world. There are several variations on the game, but in the Basque Country it is most commonly played on a court with two walls. Traditionally, it was played against the wall of the local church – and country churches still erect signs (usually ignored) forbidding the game.

of San Sebastián (*see* 'Festivals', p20). The city's best museum is the Museo San Telmo, set in a 16th-century monastery. It has recently undergone a massive restoration programme and will be reopening in 2010.

Bahía de la Concha beach

Walk: Around Donostia-San Sebastián

This short amble around the heart of Donostia-San Sebastián will introduce you to its most emblematic sights, from the stunning beach to the atmospheric Parte Vieja, and includes a bridge, a bullring, a market and a whole street full of tapas bars (Calle 31 de Agosto).

Allow a couple of hours for the walk, which is only about 1.5km (1 mile) long.

Start the walk at the Estación del Norte.

1 Estación del Norte (Northern Train Station)
The pretty station boasts an elaborate wrought-iron canopy created by Gustav Eiffel's company in the latter half of the 19th century.

2 Puente María Cristina (María Cristina Bridge)
Opposite the station is this lavishly decorated bridge, built in 1893 and adorned with four monumental obelisks. *Stroll across the bridge to the circular Plaza Bilbao, and continue straight ahead to reach the Plaza del Buen Pastor. Turn left.*

3 Catedral del Buen Pastor (Cathedral of the Good Shepherd)
This splendid neo-Gothic construction was completed in 1897. *From the Plaza del Buen Pastor, turn down Calle Urbieta to reach the seafront at Plaza Cervantes.*

4 Plaza Cervantes and seafront
From here, you can gaze out across the gorgeous curve of La Concha beach. *Turn right, towards a small, formal garden, the Jardines de Alderdi-Eder.*

5 Ayuntamiento (Town Hall)
Overlooking the garden is the golden casino, a lavish building erected in 1887. It became the Town Hall when gambling was made illegal in 1924. *Just behind the Town Hall, the Alameda del Boulevard stretches northeast.*

6 Alameda del Boulevard
Take a stroll down the boulevard to admire the wrought-iron bandstand, and perhaps stop for coffee or ice cream. *At the end, on the right, is the theatre.*

7 Teatro Victoria Eugenia (Victoria Eugenia Theatre)
Donostia's opulent, 19th-century theatre hosts the Film Festival. *Return to the Alameda and pop into the Mercado de la Bretxa.*

8 Mercado de la Bretxa (La Bretxa Market)

The municipal covered market is a great place to get picnic supplies.

From the market, plunge into the oldest and most atmospheric neighbourhood in Donostia, the Parte Vieja. Take buzzy little Calle de San Juan down to Calle Fermín Calbeton, and turn left. After one block, turn right, down Calle Narrica, and turn left. An arch on the left leads to the Plaza de la Constitución.

9 Plaza de la Constitución (Constitution Square)

This beautiful enclosed square once functioned as a bullring.

Return to the Calle Narrica and turn left to reach Calle 31 de Agosto.

10 Calle 31 de Agosto

This is the only street to emerge virtually unscathed from the last of three great fires that consumed Donostia-San Sebastián.

Walk: Around Donostia-San Sebastián

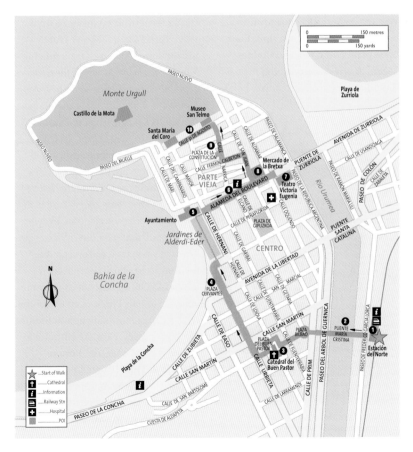

Gernika-Lumo

Gernika-Lumo holds a sacred place in Basque history. It was here, under an ancient oak tree, that the representatives of each of the seven historic Basque provinces would meet in assembly to agree laws, and where the kings of Castille later swore to uphold the ancient Basque rights, called *fueros*.

It was precisely for its symbolic importance to the Basques that General Franco chose Gernika for one of the most chilling events in the Spanish Civil War. On 26 April 1937, the town was bombarded for more than three hours by 59 planes from the Nazi Condor Legion. It was market day and the town was full. Splinter and incendiary bombs were used for maximum devastation, and the fleeing civilians were strafed with machine-guns. The world reacted with shock and horror, and Picasso was moved to paint his masterpiece *Guernica (1937)*, which hangs in the Reina Sofía Museum in Madrid.

Now the town has become a centre for peace studies and its main attraction is the **Museo de la Paz** (Peace Museum), a modern museum which recounts the town's history and includes an audio-visual exhibit that re-creates the terrible events of 26 April 1937 (*Foru Plaza 1. Tel: 946 27 02 13. www.museodelapaz.org. Open: Jul–Aug Tue–Sat 10am–8pm, Sun 10am–3pm; Sept–Jun Tue–Sat 10am–2pm & 4–7pm, Sun 10am–2pm. Admission charge, but free admission Sun except in Dec, also free 30 Jan, 26 Apr, 21 Sept, 10 Dec*).

About 5km (3 miles) northeast of Gernika-Lumo are the caves of **Santimamiñe** (*near Kortezubi. Tel: 944 65 16 57. Open: daily 10am–1.30pm & 3–7pm. Visits by advance booking only: call or email santimamine@bizkaia.net*). The caves contain some outstanding prehistoric art which dates from around 15,000 BC. Since 2008, only the entrance to the caves is open to visitors, with a virtual reconstruction of the art exhibited nearby. Near the entrance to the caves is the open-site **Bosque Pintado de Oma** (Painted Forest of Oma), where artist Agustín Ibarrola has created a fantastical wonderland by painting geometric shapes, eyes and figures directly onto the tree trunks.

The ancient oak tree in Gernika is protected by a stone structure

Getaria

Steep cobbled streets lead precipitously down to the enchanting fishing port at Getaria. For all its cobbled charm, Getaria is a proper working port and not a pristine museum town. This was the birthplace of Juan Sebastián Elcano, the first person to circumnavigate the world, whose ship limped back to port in 1522 with just 18 of its original crew. Peek into the little Gothic church of San Salvador to see the famously uneven floor surface – deliberately laid this way, so locals joke, for the comfort of mariners just back from the sea. The mouthwatering scent of barbecued fish emanates from the restaurants clustered around the port, serving the day's catch from Getaria's fishing fleet. You can walk off a long lunch on the little wooded peninsula, called El Ratón (The Mouse) for its curious shape.

The terraced slopes which surround the town are traced with vines used to produce the tart *txacolí* wine – the perfect accompaniment to fresh fish.

Vineyards near Getaria

Hondarribia

The venerable city of Hondarribia (Fuenterrabía in Castilian Spanish) is spread along the southern bank of the river Bidasoa, which forms a natural border between Spain and France.

Hondarribia's old walled town occupies a small hill, and the narrow cobbled streets are lined with traditional wooden houses with beams and porticos. The main square is dominated by a resplendent 16th-century palace built for Carlos I (Charles V, Holy Roman Emperor), which is now a *parador*. There are a number of other fine palaces, including the Palacio de Zuloaga, remodelled in the 18th century and now used as a library.

Down at the port, the old fishermen's quarter of La Marina is overlooked by charming, brightly painted wooden houses with flower-filled balconies. It's the liveliest neighbourhood, with scores of tapas bars and restaurants. The glorious wide sandy beach stretches out to Cabo Higuer, a wild headland with a lighthouse at its tip.

Cabo de Matxitxako

The lighthouse at the tip of the remote Matxitxako headland has long been the first sight of land for sailors. The waters are notoriously treacherous, littered with shipwrecks, and the stunning cliffs have been pounded into islands, caves and tunnels by the sea.

On the eastern flank of the cape, the cove of Gaztelugatxe contains a little islet connected to the mainland by a narrow bridge. It's crowned by a small sanctuary, the 10th-century **Ermita de San Juan de Gaztelugatxe**, a place of pilgrimage for sailors whose lives have been saved by invoking the saint, and the tiny chapel contains numerous ex-votos (*Open: Holy Week, Jul & Aug daily 11am–6pm. Free admission*).

Particularly popular with surfers, the little summer resort of **Bakio** is tucked around a delightful cove, and **Bermeo**,

BASQUE CUISINE

The Basques are famous throughout Spain for the excellence of their cuisine, and the region boasts the greatest concentration of Michelin-starred restaurants in the world. Superb local produce is key to traditional Basque dishes, but also to the outstanding contemporary cuisine for which local chefs such as Juan Mari Arzak, Karlos and Eva Arguiñano, and Martín Berasategui have become famous. Basque tapas (called *pintxos*) are one of the great glories of Spanish cuisine, and one of the biggest attractions of this region is joining in with the locals for the *tapeo* (a bar crawl between tapas bars).

on the other side of the headland, is the largest town in these parts, with a colourful harbour and a slew of excellent seafood restaurants. The best surfing beaches in Northern Spain can be found just east at the enticing village of **Mundaka**.

Sculptures in the park at the Chillida-Leku Museoa

The rooftops of Oñati

Chillida-Leku Museoa

A serene 16th-century country house of cool grey stone, set amid fields and woods, has been converted into a beautiful museum dedicated to the works of the celebrated Basque artist Eduardo Chillida, born in Donostia-San Sebastián in 1924. Although his earliest works were more figurative, Chillida is best known for his monumental public sculptures, such as his *Peine del Viento XV* ('Comb of the Wind') in Donostia-San Sebastián (*see p70*). He was awarded virtually every major prize in the art world, and is probably Spain's best-known contemporary artist.

The interior of the house contains galleries where the more delicate sculptures – those made of wood or alabaster, for example – are kept. The huge gardens, with their mature trees, are a breathtaking setting for around 40 larger pieces made of iron, steel and granite.

Calle Jáuregui 66, Hernani. Tel: 943 33 60 06. www.museochillidaleku.com. Open: Sept–Jun Wed–Sat & Mon 10.30am–3pm, Sun 10.30am–3pm; Jul–Aug Mon–Sat 10.30am–8pm, Sun 10.30am–3pm. Closed: Sept–Jun Tue. Admission charge.

Oñati and the Santuario de Nuestra Señora de Aránzazu

An elegant little university town, Oñati sits in a lush valley. From the 13th century it was ruled by the Guevara family, who were the counts and overlords of the region. It was here, in 1543, that the first university in the Basque Country was founded. The Renaissance university building, with its exquisite cloister, remains the town's most outstanding monument.

However, the most famous sight in Oñati is up in the hills: the Santuario de Nuestra Señora de Aránzazu, a mountain sanctuary built to commemorate the appearance of the Virgin here in 1496. The Virgin of Aránzazu is the patron saint of the province, and there has been a sanctuary here for more than 500 years. The current edifice is a grim concrete construction, erected in the 1950s, but the setting is stunning.

Santuario de Loiola

Azpeitia is an attractive Basque town set in beautiful hills, which has entered the history books thanks to its most famous son: Íñigo López de Loiola, also known as Ignatius of Loyola, born here in 1491. The house, in which the saint was born, has been incorporated into an enormous sanctuary, now one of the most important pilgrim sites in Spain. It's

The mists descend on the Santuario de Loiola

dominated by the enormous basilica, one of the finest Baroque buildings in Spain, whose dazzling interior is a magnificent whirl of gilt and marble. The elegant 15th-century mansion, where Ignatius and his 11 siblings were born, is now a museum called the Casa Santa (Holy House). It was in a room here (now called the Chapel of Conversion) that Loiola, recovering from terrible injuries inflicted during battle, had his profound religious experience. *Tel: 943 02 50 00. Open: Tue–Sat 10am–12.30pm & 3–6.15pm, Sun & public holidays 10am–12.30pm. Admission charge.*

Vitoria-Gasteiz

The capital of the Basque Country is an engaging modern city with a charming historic core, extensive public parks and an excellent reputation for its atmospheric tapas bars and restaurants.

Casco Viejo (Old Centre)

A pair of squares introduce Vitoria's delightful Old Centre: the little Plaza de la Virgen Blanca, overlooked by the grand Town Hall (Ayuntamiento), which is the heart of the city; and the much grander, enclosed and perfectly symmetrical Plaza de España. The magnificent 13th-century Catedral de Santa María is still undergoing a long-term restoration (*visits are possible by guided tour which must be booked in advance, see www.catedralvitoria.com*). There are several interesting museums, including the **Museo de Arqueología** (Archaeology Museum), which has recently moved into a stunning, bronze-clad new building designed by Patxi Mangado (*Calle Cuchilleria 54. Tel: 945 20 37 07. Open: Tue–Fri 11am–2pm & 4–6.30pm, Sat 10am–2pm, Sun 11am–2pm. Free admission*). On the edge of the Old Centre, the city's most striking contemporary building, the **Artium** (*Calle Francia 24. Tel: 945 20 90 00. www.artium.org. Open: Tue–Fri 11am–8pm, Sat–Sun & public holidays 10.30am–8pm. Admission charge*) is devoted to Basque contemporary art.

Other sights

There are two interesting museums set down a leafy path near the lovely green Parque de la Florida: the **Museo de Bellas Artes** (Fine Arts Museum), housed in an exquisite Renaissance palace (*Paseo de Fray Francisco 8. Tel: 945 18 19 18. Open: Tue–Fri 10am–2pm & 4–6.30pm, Sat 10am–2pm, Sun 11am–2pm. Free admission*), and the **Museo de la Armería de Álava** (Álava Armoury Museum) containing a collection of historic weaponry (*Paseo de Fray Francisco 3. Tel: 945 18 19 25. Open: Tue–Fri 10am–2pm & 4–6.30pm, Sat 10am–2pm, Sun 11am–2pm. Free admission*).

El Portalón is an example of medieval architecture in Vitoria

Navarra

Navarra is probably the most diverse of the Northern Spanish regions. From the dry south to Pamplona's green, river-crossed basin and the mountainous north, there is a rich variety of landscape. And, while the Navarran Pyrenees may not reach the literal heights of their neighbours in Aragón, they are equally impressive and provide a gentler range of activities and pastimes which the nature-worshipping locals pursue with a great deal of zeal.

Navarra is dotted with characterful villages, many of them perpetually filled with pilgrims on the road to Santiago de Compostela. This tiny region (10,300sq km/3,980sq miles) is divided into three, visually distinct sub-regions – the Montaña, where the Pyrenees dominate the landscape, the lush basin of the Zona Media, and the hotter, drier more 'Spanish' Ribera in the south – and is cradled by the borders of La Rioja, to the north by France and to the west by the Basque Country. In the 10th century, the powerful Kingdom of Navarra was born out of the *Reconquista* (the Christian conquest of Spain against the Moors) and encompassed swathes of these lands. Even today, extreme Basque nationalists would like to see Navarra return to the Basque fold; Basque culture and language is prominent, particularly in the isolated rural villages of the north.

The Navarrans are a welcoming people, evidently proud of their beautiful homeland and eager to share its assets with the rest of the world (Navarra's network of tourist information offices is among the most organised and helpful in Spain). Add this to its stunning natural landscape, fabulous cuisine and rich artistic heritage, and you have a cocktail that's hard to beat.

Bardenas Reales and Tudela

The drier, southernmost swathe of Navarra has less of the stunning beauty that characterises the mountainous north, with one notable exception: the incredible Bardenas Reales.

Strictly speaking a semi-arid desert, the Bardenas Reales is a natural park with a 42,500-hectare (105,000-acre) extent, consisting of the most surreal, lunar-esque landscape imaginable. Centuries of wind and erosion have created the most remarkable plateaus, natural terraces, rocks, cliffs, crags and ravines you are likely to see on the planet. Driving though the desert, it's hard not to blink twice. Decaying fortresses, molten pyramids, bulbous towers – and yes, the odd extraterrestrial – seem to morph out of the clay, limestone and gypsum. To the north are the Plateau de Bardenas and the Bardena Blanca, a majestic series of grey-white gypsum cliffs, while to the south is the Bardena Negra, with tatty pine forests and red clay mounds hugging the ground in mesmerising formations. In between is a relentless, dry landscape that sort of pummels you into submission with its sheer, naturally formed strangeness.

Equally odd is the area's history. When Navarra was a kingdom, this no-man's land acted as a buffer zone between Moorish invaders and the Navarran armies, the latter of which was largely manned by peasant farmers. In 882, the monarchs granted the inhabitants of the villages dotted around the Bardenas special rights as a

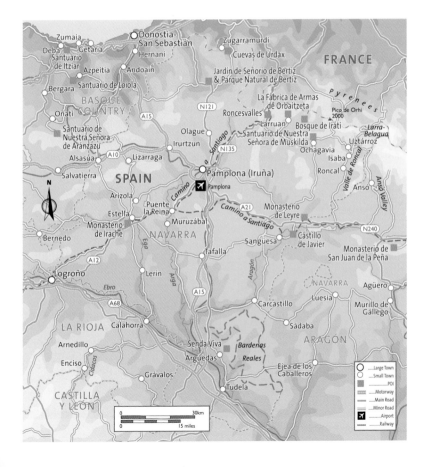

way of thanks, letting them herd their flocks on the land once snow hit the northern valleys. These rights have not only remained but increased, and today 22 communities 'manage' the desert by Royal Decree. They are still the only people to have grazing rights, and they earn extra money by renting out the land for film shoots (it has been used as a location for the James Bond film *The World is Not Enough*) and hunting permits.

The extreme harshness of the Bardenas Reales limits activities to gentle walking, cycling and driving through in your car. There is one hotel within the park (*see p179*), so most visitors stay in Tudela. Here, the **tourist information office** can provide you with maps and information (*Calle Juicio 4. Tel: 948 84 80 58. Open: Mon–Fri 9.30am–2pm & 4–8pm, Sat 10am–2pm & 4–8pm, Sun 10am–2pm*).

Tudela itself is an elegant town on the Ebro river, famous for its *cogollos*

(cos lettuce hearts); you'll see them on restaurant menus everywhere, often simply accompanied by Cantabrian anchovies and olive oil. Head first to the buzzing Plaza de los Fueros, where bullfights used to be held (there are bull-related carvings on the surrounding buildings), then take a stroll to the cathedral. Built on the site of the old mosque (which was destroyed during the *Reconquista*), it boasts three richly carved portals and a tranquil Romanesque cloister.

If you are travelling with children – and the Bardenas Reales is wonderful for kids – **Senda Viva** is a good side excursion. Located near the village of Arguedas, it's a cross between a zoo, natural park and theme park, with some hair-raising rides and lots of cuddly animals to ogle (*Tel: 948 08 81 00. www.sendaviva.com. Generally open: Thur–Sun 10am–7pm, but check he website or call first*).

The desert landscape of Bardenas Reales

LA FÁBRICA DE ARMAS DE ORBAITZETA

Deep in the Irati forest, the ruins of the old arms factory of Orbaitzeta is a surprisingly fascinating place to wander around. Abandoned more than a century ago, it was once the largest military installation in all of Spain, drawing on the area's rich deposits of iron, silver and lead. It was attacked various times throughout its history, including by Napoleon in the War of Independence (1808), but parts of the workers' cottages, deposits, ovens and water tunnel remain. Much of it has been occupied by the Irati's verdant plant life, which provides a thought-provoking metaphor of the power of nature over man. *From Orbaitzeta, look for the signs to LarrE
a few kilometres further north towards France. This is the location of the factory.*

Bosque de Irati

If Venus were a forest she would be Irati. This stunningly beautiful gift from Mother Nature is spread over nearly 18 hectares (44 acres), mainly in the Aezkoa and Salazar valleys but also into France. It is a lush, magical place, thick with oak, chestnut, fir, maple and particularly giant beech trees. Fauna includes the ubiquitous *jabalí* (wild boar), foxes, squirrels and thousands of migrating birds resting in Irati's verdant folds. Within the borders of the forest are three nature reserves, waterfalls, gorges, a lake, springs and the eerie remains of a weapons factory (*see box above*). At its northernmost flank the forest meets the mountains; at 2,000m (6,560ft), the Pico de Orhi is the highest, and from the top affords panoramic views of the valleys below. Needless to say, the forest is a magnet for walkers, cyclists and, in winter, cross-country skiers. But such is the extent of the Irati that even gentle strolls can be had from its various entry points. A popular one is from Ochagavia (*see p87*). Follow the NA2012 up the mountain from the village. At the entrance to the forest, follow the marked footpaths (there is a small information point here in summer only; alternatively, pick up a map from the tourist information office in Ochagavia). The shortest route, which takes about an hour, ends at a lovely waterfall.

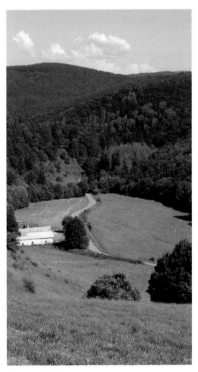

Bosque de Irati

Estella and the Monasterio de Irache

While many hospices, monasteries, churches and bridges were constructed along the Camino a Santiago to aid pilgrims, Estella (or Lizarra) has the distinction of being built entirely from the ground up in order to attract them. But despite its touristy beginnings (and its rather lofty title as the 'Toledo of the North'), Estella today is a likeable, work-a-day place with a clutch of attractions and services that may make you linger longer than expected.

The Argo river divides the town. On its western bank is the imposing Iglesia de San Pedro de la Rua, standing in lofty stateliness at the top of a disconcerting number of stone stairs (worth climbing for the 13th-century portal carved with plants and figurines). Opposite, at ground level, is the **Palacio de los Reyes de Navarra**, which, as the royal palace, has the distinction of being the only secular Romanesque edifice in Navarra (*Tel: 948 55 63 01. Open: Mon–Sat 10am–2pm & 4–7pm, Sun 10am–2pm*). Inside are the information office and pilgrims info point, and a gallery containing the works of the painter Gustavo de Maeztu (1887–1947).

If the west bank is crawling with dishevelled-looking pilgrims, the eastern one is where the smart locals live, work and above all shop (trade was an important activity for the early pilgrims, and it seems business has not let up since). They hang out and have coffee at the Plaza de los Fueros, a wide square dominated by the Iglesia de San Juan and some fine medieval mansions.

Just outside Estella, the 11th-century Monasterio de Irache is another important stop along the Camino a Santiago. It was the first hospice in the region to be built specially for the pilgrims, who still stop here to quench their thirst from two taps from the monastery's *bodega*: one dispensing water and the other wine. The monastery can be toured, including access to the Baroque tower, the 12th-century church and Plateresque-style cloister (*Open: Tue 9am–1pm, Wed–Fri 9am–1.30pm & 5–7pm, Sat & Sun 9am–1.30pm & 4–7pm. Free admission*).

Palacio de los Reyes de Navarra

Fountain and lily pond at the Jardín de Señorio de Bertiz

Jardín de Señorio de Bertiz and the Parque Natural de Bertiz

Truly beautiful public gardens are rare in Spain, making the Jardín de Señorio de Bertiz a very special place. They were established by one Don Pedro Ciga in the late 19th century, who after his death left the property to the state. Ciga was an enlightened gentleman who travelled widely and had an avid interest in nature and ecology. His legacy is incredibly romantic: pergolas, fountains and water-lily-blanketed ponds have been placed among manicured plots of a diverse range of trees, flowers and shrubs, many of which were imported from abroad. His old manor house boasts some gorgeous Art Nouveau flourishes, and while access is not allowed, it is occasionally used for exhibitions.

The garden lies at the entrance to the Parque Natural de Bertiz, a 2,400-hectare (5,930-acre) woodland spread over the mountainside, thick with oak, chestnut and ash trees and peppered with waterfalls and streams. Clear signposts mark out some easy walks through the forest. Enquire at the **information office** (*Tel: 948 59 24 21*) at the entrance to the Jardín de Señorio de Bertiz. *Garden open: summer 10am–8pm; winter 10am–6pm. Admission charge.*

Monasterio de Leyre

Located alone on a limestone cliff overlooking a reservoir, the Leyre Monastery is an evocative place. Over the centuries it has served as royal court, an Episcopal seat and the pantheon for the kings of Navarra.

Leyre is still a working monastery, inhabited by a community of monks who perform Gregorian chants daily to the general public (*at 7.30am, 9am & 7pm*). Only two parts of the complex are accessible to mere mortals, but their beauty is well worth the detour.

The first, opposite the ticket office (which sells CDs of the monks' chants along with other notable religious kitsch) is the crypt, the oldest part of the complex. It's an eerie space, with fat, squat quartz columns and eye-level capitals carved with rudimentary figures, all bathed in a disturbing nicotine-coloured artificial light. After some time here, you will be

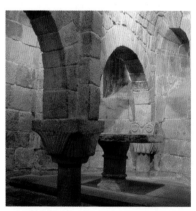

The atmospheric crypt at the Monasterio de Leyre

handed keys to the church (access is controlled). Before you go in, stop a while outside to take in its marvellous carved portal, which features biblical scenes and beasts typically Romanesque and familiar to those following the Santiago route (the monastery is a stop-off). The Gothic arches of the interior are remarkably well executed and austere, and a large casket adjacent to the wall contains the bones of ten Navarran monarchs.

Open: Mon–Fri 10.15am–2pm & 3.30–7pm. Admission charge.

Ochagavia

This little village, nestled in the folds of the Salazar Valley, is as pretty as a picture. Six pert stone bridges cross the Anduña river, and on either side prim stone town houses with blazing flower boxes sit in neat rows. Some have been turned into guesthouses, and there is a campsite to the north of the town, making Ochagavia a good base from which to explore the wonderful Irati forest (*see p83*) which lies 24km (15 miles) up the mountain. In the village, an **information office** about the forest can fix you up with maps and walking routes (*Open: summer Mon–Sat 10am–2pm & 4.30–8.30pm, Sun 10am–2pm; winter weekends only*).

There are two churches in Ochagavia worth seeking out. The first, in the village itself, is the 12th-century Iglesia de San Juan Evangelista that contains three fine Renaissance altarpieces. The second, located 4km (2½ miles) outside

Ochagavia, is the lovely Santuario de Nuestra Señora de Muskilda. Every year on 8 September, Ochagavia's *danzantes* (traditional dancers) make a pilgrimage here in an event filled with colour, gaiety and music.

Pamplona (Iruña)

Navarra's capital is an engaging place, known the world over for its famous 'Running of the Bulls' festival (*see pp88–9*). Pamplona's Casco Antiguo (Old Centre) is compact and best seen on foot (*see 'Walk', pp90–91*), though its largest monument lies slightly out of the centre in the Ensanche (or 'Extension') neighbourhood. The star-shaped Ciudadela (Citadel) was ordered by King Felipe II in 1571, not only to keep an eye on French invaders but also uprisings from the city itself, which a few decades earlier (along with the rest of the old Kingdom of Navarra) had been forcibly united with Castile by Fernando de Aragón.

Surrounded by lush green parkland, the citadel is an agreeable place to visit whether you are interested in military architecture or not. At most times of the day it is filled with joggers and cyclists, and the grass-filled interior of the citadel is now used for outdoor cultural events.

Puente la Reina

Little Puente la Reina is named after the humped stone bridge spanning the River Argo, which was built for pilgrims back in the 11th century. The village is

The Anduña river in Ochagavia

still a major stop on the Santiago Way, and most modern-day pilgrims can be seen around the Calle Major, where a clutch of bars and hostels are located (the Plaza Julian Mena is the most picturesque place to rest up on one of the terrace-cafés). Many make a side excursion to Muruzábal, a hamlet located five kilometres to the southeast. Here lies the **Church of Santa Maria de Eunate** (*open: Jan, Feb & Dec Tue–Sun 10.30am–2.30pm; Mar–Jun & Oct 10.30am–1.30pm, 4–7pm; Jul–Sept 10.30am–1.30pm, 5–8pm. Free admission*), a harmonious, 12th century octagonal structure standing alone in the middle of a field. Its purpose remains somewhat of a mystery; some say it was built as a hospital of the Templar Knights, others say it was a church for Santiago's pilgrims, although its location off the main route throws doubt on this.

Los Sanfermínes
(The Running of the Bulls)

Undoubtedly Spain's most internationally-known festival, Los Sanfermínes is either loved or loathed (even by the locals). But it should probably figure high on the list of spectacles to see just once in your life.

San Fermín is the patron saint of Navarra and the party starts on 6 July – his designated Saint's Day. The whole town – plus thousands of tourists lucky enough to find a hotel room or at least pay the exorbitant prices they are charging – gathers outside the Town Hall sporting red and white neck scarves, the traditional garb of the nine-day fiesta.

Poster advertising the bull running

At midday the mayor fires a rocket from the Town Hall balcony, marking the opening of the event to deafening cries of 'Viva San Fermín!'.

And live they do – to the fullest. From then on, it's non-stop mayhem; a party that gets progressively wilder as the days wear on. Music rings out (loudly) from every bar well into the night, most frequented by packs of frat boys determined to stay up until the daily 'runnings' (or *encierros*) at 8am. Yet, despite the huge tourist presence, Los Sanfermínes has a genuine local feel to it, with religious processions, live singing and dancing and plenty of local colour. In the cool of the evening whole families take to the streets to simply enjoy their city.

You can still see the major sites (in fact, with most the city sleeping off the night before, it's a good opportunity to do so), though you will find that services such as banks are in first gear, and some smaller establishments simply pull down the shutters and close shop for the week. Animal activists should take note that you can go the entire time without so much as smelling a bull (and you will know it when you do).

A statue showing the drama of the Running of the Bulls

The bulls run along a designated route of the impossibly narrow, cobblestoned streets in the old town, which are barricaded off to the public by wooden fences. The starting point is the bulls' iron-gated corral, where men (and some women) brave or silly enough wait outside ready to run ahead of them as soon as the gate goes up. The danger, say the experts, comes from the twists and turns of the route, where runners can slip over and risk being trampled on, or a bull loses itself from the herd and becomes disoriented and aggressive. After the death of a young American runner in 1995, local police have been more vigilant about who they let participate, and anyone seemingly inexperienced or inebriated will be pulled out of the crowd and told to sit it out.

The whole thing happens in the bat of an eye, and you'll need to be high up, whether hanging from a lamppost or sitting on a private balcony, to see it (you can hire one for the occasion; visit *www.sanfermin.com*). A more comfortable option is buying a ticket for the Plaza del Toros (*www.feriadeltoro.com*), which is where the *encierros* end. The sight of a crowd of red-and-white-clad *sanfermineros* pelting into the ring at full speed followed by a stampede of these magnificent creatures is a sight you won't forget in a hurry.

Walk: Around Pamplona

The vestiges of Pamplona's Roman roots and defensive role as a border town throughout history can all be seen on a stroll around its ancient neighbourhoods.

Allow an hour for the 1.5km (under a mile) covered – or two if you plan to visit the Museo de Navarra.

Start your walk in the Plaza del Castillo in the centre of Pamplona's handsome Casco Antiguo. For drivers, there is a handy underground car park.

1 Plaza del Castillo

On the southern flank of the square is the stately Diputación, or Seat of the Government of Navarra. On the opposite side is the famous Café Iruña, an elegant bar-café where the writer Ernest Hemingway was a regular (his novel *The Sun Also Rises* was set in Pamplona). He is honoured with a statue at the entrance. *Take Calle Chapitela northwards to the Plaza Consistorial.*

2 Ayuntamiento (City Hall)

Pamplona's frothy Baroque City Hall sits at the intersection of three ancient neighbourhoods: Navarrería, San Santurnino and San Nicolás. The square becomes awash with people at the start of the San Fermín festival (*see pp88–9*). *Take Calle Curia northeast to the Plaza San José.*

3 La Catedral de Santa María (Cathedral of St Mary)

The imposing façade of Pamplona's cathedral is neoclassical, but inside are

many Gothic elements, and the tombs of King Carlos III of Navarra and his wife. The cathedral houses a **Museo Diocesano** with sacred art from all over Navarra (*Open: mid-Jun–mid-Sept Mon–Sat 10am–7pm, Sun 11am–2pm; mid-Sept–mid-Jun Mon–Fri 10am–2pm & 4–7pm, Sat 10am–2pm*). *Leave via Calle Navarrería, take the first right then left into Calle Dos de Mayo.*

4 Palacio de los Reyes de Navarra (Palace of the Kings of Navarra)

This old palace holds the archives of the province and has been given a makeover by Navarran Pritzker-Prize-winning architect Rafael Moneo. *Continue in the same direction along Calle Dos de Mayo.*

5 Museo de Navarra (Navarra Museum)

This museum is located inside the former hospital of Nuestra Señora de la Misericordia and contains works from across the region (*Open: Tue–Sat*

9.30am–2pm & 5–7pm, Sun 11am–2pm. Admission charge).
Walk to the rear of the museum towards the Arga river.

6 Murallas (walls)

Pamplona's walls were erected in the early 1500s as the Spanish monarchy increasingly relied on the city to defend Spain against the French.
From Calle Descalzos, take Calle Hilarion Eslava, passing the Plaza de San Francisco and turning into Calle San Miguel. Stop at the corner of Calle de San Nicolás.

7 Iglesia de San Nicolás (Church of St Nicholas)

This has been the religious epicentre of the neighbourhood since the 12th

century and bridges both Gothic and Romanesque styles. Inside is an extravagant Baroque organ, and outside are porticos from a later period.
Backtrack to the Plaza de San Francisco, and diagonally cross the square to Calle Ansoleaga and turn right.

8 Iglesia de San Saturnino (Church of St Saturnino)

This church is allegedly built on the spot where Bishop Saturnino baptised thousands of local pagans. Its weather vane, the Gallico de San Cernín, has become a symbol of Pamplona. Inside is a beautiful 12th-century statue of the Virgin Mary.
Return to Calle San Nicolás to refuel in one of its buzzing tapas bars.

Walk: Around Pamplona

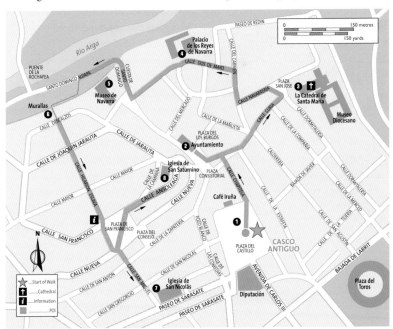

Roncesvalles

The beautiful mountain pass of Roncesvalles (or Oreaga) has always held a significant place in Navarra's history. It is the first stop for pilgrims following the French route on the Camino a Santiago, and it was here, in the 8th century, that many of King Charlemagne's armies fell during his campaign to hold back the Moors and unite Western Europe. One of them was the knight Roland, a heroic fighter mythologised in the epic poem *Le Chanson de Roland* (though in all probability it was the feisty Basques, not the Moors, he was rallying against when he died).

But it was the discovery of St James' tomb in Santiago de Compostela in Galicia that put this tiny outpost on the map. A pilgrim hostel sprouted up in 1127, followed shortly after by a church that has morphed into the enormous **Colegiata de Santa María** complex, a hotchpotch of styles and elements that attracts pilgrims and religious tourists like bees to a honey pot (*Open: 10am–2pm & 3.30–7pm. Admission charge*). This is not to say it's without its merits: the late Gothic Chapel of St Agustín – the resting place of King Sancho VII ('the strong') – is superb. Above his alabaster tomb is a stained-glass depiction of the dashing monarch leading the famous Battle of Tolosa against the Moors. The pride of the collegiate, however, is in the lovely French Gothic church: the silver-plated Virgen de Roncesvalles, allegedly found in the area by a shepherd guided to the spot by a vision, an event celebrated every 8 September with a moving *romería* (or pilgrimage festival).

There is not much of a 'village' in Roncesvalles, more a handful of hostels and restaurants catering to the constant stream of pilgrims. The countryside, however, is heavenly and there is good walking to be had in the vicinity, and a couple of picnic spots. Enquire at the tourist information office near the entrance to the collegiate.

Colegiata de Santa María, Roncesvalles

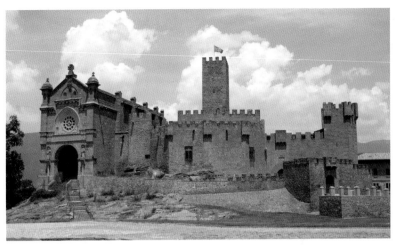

The Castillo de Javier looks like something out of a fantasy film

Sangüesa and the Castillo de Javier

Like Estella (*see p84*), Sangüesa is a town that owes its prosperity to the Navarran leg of the Camino a Santiago. In the 12th century, much of the pilgrim-related activity, particularly trade, was centred around the Calle Mayor and so, today, are its most important monuments. The 13th-century church Santiago del Mayor has a precious figurine of St James above its portal, a popular photo opportunity for contemporary pilgrims. Santa María Real Church, also from the same period, has a superbly carved portal featuring the last judgement, and the Convento de San Francisco de Asís (it is believed the saint visited the town upon his return from Santiago de Compostela) is a moving single-nave structure from the 16th century. For a change of pace, seek out the Palacio de Vallesantoro (now the Town Hall). This riot of a building contains every Baroque piece of frippery imaginable on its façade.

A few kilometres from Sangüesa, the impressive Castillo de Javier, dating from the 11th century but with later additions, is located on the birthplace of St Francis Javier (or Xabier), founder of the Jesuit order. There is a college and a couple of hotels and restaurants on its manicured lawns, along with the predictable souvenir shops and parking for tourist buses. But focus on the castle itself, which can be visited inside and is particularly fun for children (even better for fans of *Harry Potter*), with battlements to climb, displays of medieval artefacts and some scary skeleton murals in the chapel.

Castillo de Javier. Tel: 948 88 40 24. Open: 10am–1.30pm & 3.30–6.30pm. Admission charge.

Navarra

Valle de Roncal and Belagua

In the Roncal Valley, you may notice a larger-than-usual (even for Spain) number of fluffy white sheep grazing on the lush green hillsides. That is because enchanting Roncal is famous for its eponymous cheese, which is sold all over the region (*see box*). But there are many more reasons to visit the valley, the easternmost in Navarra. Here is where the Navarran Pyrenees really start to display their majesty, making it a wonderful place for cross-country skiers and walkers. And you'll be entranced by the sheer charm of the villages that dot the region.

Foremost is Roncal, where cobblestoned streets wind up the mountain as far as gravity allows and traditional town houses sport immaculately kept *huertas* (vegetable gardens). One has been turned into the **Casa-Museo Gayarre** (*Open: Apr–Sept Tue–Sun 11.30am–1.30pm & 5–7pm; Oct–Mar Sat & Sun 11.30am–1.30pm &*

RONCAL CHEESE

Yet another charming Roncalese village is Uztárroz, located between Roncal and Isaba. If it's local cheese you are craving, you have come to the right place. The nutty, golden-coloured sheep's-milk Roncal cheese was the first in Spain to earn a DO (*Denominación de Orígin*), meaning that, as with French champagne, no other maker outside the region can name their product as such, and production must adhere to strict standards. In Uztárroz, a local cheesemaker has set up a rather charming museum explaining his craft, and the delicious fruits of his labour are sold on site.

Museo del Queso. Open: Mon–Fri 8.30am–1.30pm, Sat noon–2pm & 4–6pm, Sun noon–2pm. Free admission.

4–5pm. Admission charge). Local lad Julián Gayarre started life as a shepherd. In the 19th century he found considerable fame as a tenor in the theatres of Madrid and across Europe. In 1889 he ended his career with a fittingly operatic flourish. During a performance, his voice cracked, though he did manage to squeak out the words, 'I can't sing any more'. He died 25 days later and is buried in an elaborate tomb in Roncal's cemetery.

A little further north, Isaba is the valley's largest village, and the closest to Belagua on the French border. While not quite as bewitching as Roncal, it has a good range of accommodation and services and is a popular base, especially if you plan to do any mountain-related activities or nip over the border for the sheer thrill of it. France's shepherds have done so for

Roncal village

A view up the Belagua Valley

centuries, leading their flocks to greener and wetter Roncal pastures. You can still see a handful of these hardy souls criss-crossing the Belagua Valley, which adjoins the northernmost tip of the Roncal Valley.

Belagua is the only glacial valley in Navarra and is dotted with pines, hazelnut trees, oaks and firs, and is popular for skiing in the winter. At its northernmost extreme lies the Reserva de Larra, an awe-inspiring plateau 2,500m (8,200ft) above sea level and surrounded by the peaks of the mountains of Anie, Arias and Lakora. It is a privileged area for hiking, where you may spot Camille, the only surviving bear in the area, among the marmots and horses. Every 13 July the mayors of the Barétous Valley in France meet at the border to present the authorities of Belagua with three cows in thanks for the use of their water sources – a quaint ceremony that goes back to 1375.

Zugarramurdi

This tiny, pretty stone village in the deep north of Navarra combines natural beauty with a fascinating history. Its main attractions are the so-called 'Witches' Caves', eerily beautiful, formed by a 120m-long (130 yard) natural tunnel containing various rocky platforms and terraces (*Open: 9am–dusk. Admission charge*). During the 17th century, the dark days of the Spanish Inquisition, they were allegedly the meeting place for witches' covens, a rumour not unnoticed by the

Looking towards the Reserva de Larra

The Witches' Caves at Zugarramurdi

authorities in Logroño (now La Rioja, see p107), who sent in a task force to hunt down the 'witches' (predictably single and aging women, but also men) and convert them to Christianity – often by heinous torture methods (see box). History aside (though it's hard to ignore the location's disturbing past), the caves are a fascinating place. Take the time to wander around their periphery along the clearly marked paths that lead through thick forest, along streams, and up to a good view.

Zugarramurdi itself is a lovely place to linger, with a medieval plaza dominated by the 18th-century Iglesia de Asunción and a handful of decent bars and eateries. A few kilometres south, the **Cuevas de Urdax** are another fascinating wonder of nature, with caves stretching nearly 2,000sq m (21,500sq ft) and containing various 'rooms' of impressive stalactites (*Tel: 948 59 92 41. Admission charge, guided visits only*).

THE WITCHES OF ZUGARRAMURDI

When rumours of black magic and witchcraft in Zugarramurdi reached the ears of the head honchos of the Spanish Inquisition in 1610, they sent *inquisidor* Don Juan del Valle Alvarado to investigate. After spending months gathering 'evidence' (much of it based on hearsay), he accused more than 300 villagers of crimes ranging from attending black masses to having sexual intercourse with a goat. Forty (including children) were sent to Logroño to languish in prisons, while 12 were burnt at the stake. The excellent **Museo de Brujas**, located close to the caves in Zugarramurdi, is a moving tribute to these souls and an excellent introduction to local myth and legend (*Tel: 948 59 90 04. Open: winter Wed–Fri 11am–6pm, Sat & Sun 11am–7pm; extended hours in summer. Admission charge*).

La Rioja

When most people outside Spain hear the word 'Rioja' they think of the wine. And rightly so. It is Spain's most internationally recognised export, drunk everywhere from Montreal to Melbourne. But the province of La Rioja has much more to offer: ancient villages and monasteries, stunning mountain scenery and, of course, a hands-on experience in the wonderful world of viniculture.

This compact little region (5,000sq km/ 1,930sq miles) boasts some breathtaking scenery in the Sierra de la Demanda in the south, while the north is dominated by blankets of vineyards and pretty hilltop villages. But even more than sights, La Rioja stands out for the intoxicating, centuries-old culture that has been woven around its wine – and that, for many, is more than enough.

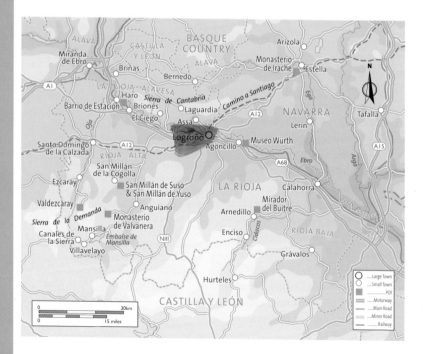

Although it lacks serious academic study, there is something to be said for the happy-go-lucky, slightly nutty disposition of people who live and work in a wine region. Riojans are no exception. As soon as you meet one you will find yourself merrily discussing the merits of this year's *crianza* (or vintage), most likely with a glass of it in hand. Riojans are fully aware of the fact that their mainstay product is the principal reason people visit their province, and they've trail-blazed wine tourism in Spain. But unlike, say, the Napa Valley or Tuscany, La Rioja is more work-a-day, with warehouses, modern industrial *bodegas* and working-class villages. Of course the snobbery that goes with a wine culture exists (particularly in the region's posh restaurants and hotels), but most Riojans, many of whom have been brewing their own backyard *vino* (wine) for generations, see it as an everyday commodity, something to be consumed without ceremony and above all shared around.

For the purposes of this book, we have included a part of the region of Álava in this chapter. Though it geographically belongs to the Basque Country, it is also the production hub of Rioja and the location of some of its most emblematic wineries.

Briones

Briones is an archetypal Rioja Alavesa village, with a pretty Baroque church (the Nuestra Señora de la Asunción) and a handful of *casonas*, noble town houses once owned by the region's rich wine burghers. But the main reason to come here is the excellent **Museo de la Cultura del Vino**, located on the edge of town as you exit the highway (*Tel: 902 32 00 01. www.dinastiavivanco.com. Open: Tue–Thur & Sun 10am–6pm, Fri & Sat 10am–8pm; ticket office closes 90 minutes before closing time. Admission charge*). It's a fascinating, state-of-the-art trip through the culture and history of winemaking in the region, covering early methods introduced by the Romans, their development by the monasteries, modern production methods and how to identify different varietals. The admission charge includes a glass of Vivanco wine.

Sculpture at the wine museum in Briones

Calahorra

Calahorra is the capital of the less-visited and less-populated Rioja Baja ('Lower Rioja') region, and while wine culture is not as pre-eminent here as in Haro (*see pp104–5*), Calahorra should appeal to lovers of history, ancient architecture and authentic Spanish towns. During the Roman reign of the peninsula, Calahorra was one of the most important cities and home to the Roman orator Quintiliano, whose statue resides proudly in Calahorra's main square.

Roman ruins are now sparse in Calahorra, bar some thoughtfully displayed in the garden outside the **tourist information office** (*Calle Angel Olivan 8. Tel: 941 10 50 61*) and some vestiges of the Roman Circus on the Paseo Mercadal. However, the town has some notable medieval attractions.

Its superb **cathedral** rises up over the Cicados river, its elegant neoclassical façade reflected in the muddy water (*Open: Mon–Sat 9am–12.45pm, Sun mass only*). Its various chapels contain elements from the Romanesque to Gothic and Renaissance movements, with the most outstanding being an intricate Plateresque *retablo* (or altarpiece) in the Capilla de San Pedro (or Chapel of St Peter). Another rich Plateresque work is on the outside of the cathedral: the delicate 16th-century Puerta de San Jerónimo on the Calle Arrabal. Also from the 16th century, the **Iglesia de San Andrés** has an equally beautiful door featuring carvings symbolising the conquest of Christianity over perceived paganism), and an ornate Rococo *retablo* and choir (*Open: Mon–Sat 6–7.30pm, Sun mass only*).

The ornate façade of Calahorra's cathedral

Skeletal display at the Centro Paleontológico

A lively market is held in Calahorra every Thursday in the Plaza de la Verdura, where local farmers bring in the fruits and vegetables from their *huertas*.

Enciso and Arnedillo

Enciso is a pretty little village with a pair of important 16th-century churches (the Santa María de la Estrella and the San Pedro) and the ruins of a castle high on the hill above it. But it's famed throughout La Rioja as Dinosaur Country. About 120 million years ago this area, which was then lush and green, was a hangout for dinosaurs, both herbivorous and carnivorous. Some of their footprints were left in a lagoon which, over the centuries, was filled with minerals and mud, dried and turned to stone. There are more than 3,000 footprints dotted around Enciso, divided into various routes. Maps can be picked up at the **Centro**

Paleontológico in Enciso (*Tel: 941 39 60 93. Open: Jun–mid-Sept 11am–2pm & 5–8pm; mid-Sept–May Mon–Sat 11am–2pm & 3–6pm, Sun 11am–2pm. Admission charge*). You can also pre-book tours of the footprints (usually at weekends).

A natural wonder of the living kind can be found in Arnedillo, a tiny hamlet 10km (6 miles) north of Enciso in the heart of the beautiful Cidacos Valley. Located in the mountains high above the Cidacos river, the **Mirador del Buitre** lets you observe a large colony of leopard vultures via a monitoring system that projects images in real time on large screens inside the *mirador* (*Tel: 941 39 42 26*). Strategically placed telescopes give you further insight into these majestic creatures. The river's waters are said to have amazing curative effects and Arnedillo also has a famed spa-hotel (*see p181*).

The wines of La Rioja

La Rioja may not be Spain's only wine region, but it is certainly its largest and most renowned. More than 500 *bodegas* (or wineries) dot the region, from humble single-vineyard operations to the razzle-dazzle structures of Frank Gehry and Santiago Calatrava (*see pp112–13*). Wherever you go, viniculture permeates everyday life, from the acres of vineyards to the thriving bar culture and wine-themed festivals.

La Rioja was Spain's first wine to receive a DO (*Denominación de Origen*, or Qualified Designation of Origin), represented by the red and

An apt fountain in Fuenmayor

white vine logo you see on the bottle. Somewhat confusingly, the DO covers wine produced in some parts of Navarra and La Rioja Alavesa, which is geographically part of the Basque country. The DO was awarded in 1902 and today three exist: La Rioja Alavesa, Rioja Alta and Rioja Baja. While these *consejos* (or sub-qualifications) denote to a certain extent the wine's style, the overwhelming majority of La Rioja wine is red, with the fruity, full-bodied *tempranillo* grape reigning supreme. Other grapes that are used to a lesser extent are *garnacha* and *graciano*. White wine using the *macabeo* grape is also produced, but rarely drums up the same enthusiasm as the region's gloriously rich reds.

Wine production in La Rioja started in the Middle Ages. As in many parts of Europe, monks, with plenty of time on their hands and a sure-fire demand every Sunday, practised winemaking from behind the high walls of their monasteries. Their knowledge was imparted to the plebeians, and many families started producing their own moonshine in rudimentary subterranean *bodegas* underneath their homes, some of which still exist (*see 'La Fabulista',*

Vineyards southeast of Briones

p112). In the 19th century the phylloxera plague wiped out most of France's vineyards, so industrious chateaux owners ventured south in search of fertile lands. They taught Riojan winemakers a thing or two about modern winemaking, and an industry was born.

Choosing wines to buy in La Rioja can be slightly daunting. As a rule of thumb remember that *crianza* (or vintage) has been aged for at least two years, *reserva* for at least one year in an oak barrel, and *gran reserva* for at least two years in oak and then three in a bottle. (You will be asked if you want a *crianza* or *reserva* when ordering a glass of wine in a bar.) The award-winners tend to come from the La Rioja Alavesa and Alta regions, where the majority of 'old vine' vineyards exist. Wines from Rioja Baja are paler and less acidic, and often have higher alcohol content. Most generic Rioja reds, however, are produced using a mixture of all three.

That said, it's a rare day when you will find a sub-standard tipple in La Rioja. Having embraced wine tourism over the past decade, most wineries, particularly those around Haro (*see pp104–5*) and Laguardia (*see pp105–6*), are open to the public, letting you taste before you buy. Some winery tours and tastings may need to be booked in advance (enquire at the tourist information offices), but smaller producers never seem to mind if you simply pull up and ask to sample their wares. ¡*Salud*!

Ezcaray

When you mention Ezcaray in these parts, most people think snow – it's the base of Valdezcaray, one of the only ski resorts in La Rioja. But even off-season it's well worth visiting, and not only because it's home to the acclaimed Hotel Echaurren and restaurant El Portal (*see pp181 & 182*).

Placed on the banks of the bubbling Oja river and surrounded by thick forests of beech and oak, Ezcaray is an enchanting place that, despite the thousands of snow bunnies who invade it every season, has remained stubbornly unchanged. Traditional stone homes with white façades and exposed woodwork line the Plaza de la Verdura, a medieval plaza with a pert little fountain in the centre. Its most important monument is the Gothic Iglesia Santa María del Mayor, a fortress-like church with two imposing cylindrical towers.

Apart from snow, Ezcaray's big claim to fame is its artisan heritage, and woodwork objects, local jams, cheeses and honeys can be found in the local shops. For centuries the town was renowned for weaving. Only one factory remains, **Hijos de Cecilio Valgañón**, and it has a shop in the centre of town selling luxurious mohair, lamb's wool and cashmere blankets and scarves at a fraction of the cost of elsewhere (*Calle Gallarza 12. Tel: 941 35 40 34. Open: Mon–Fri 9am–1pm & 3–7pm, Sat 9am–1pm & 4.30–7.30pm, Sun 10.30am–2pm*).

A BACCHANALIAN BUN FIGHT

If you find yourself near Haro on 29 June, be sure to wear a waterproof jacket. Not because it's likely to rain, but you may get deluged by litres of wine. The famous Batalla del Vino (Battle of the Wine) takes place in Riscos de San Bilibio, a hillside surrounded by vineyards a few kilometres from the town. This messy festival commemorates a regional dispute, and starts off with a church service. Afterwards, the mayor climbs to a hilltop castle in a mock act of dominance. Then the battle begins; the white-clad crowd below lets loose, and everyone is fair game. Wine spews forth from spray guns, water pistols, dustbins, buckets and everything else imaginable and, needless to say, litres of it is consumed straight up. After midday it's back to Haro for a triumphant march around the main square, with fireworks and more festivities in the evening.

Haro

Capital of La Rioja Alta and epicentre of La Rioja's winemaking industry, Haro practically lives and breathes *vino* – and after a day or so here, you may find that you do too. Most of the *bodegas* are clustered around the Barrio de Estación, so named because of railway station and line that was built in order to export its product to the rest of Europe. One of the most emblematic is López de Heredia's **Viña Tondonia** (*see p113*), a 132-year-old winery with a labyrinth of underground aging tunnels and a distinctive russet-red tower. Another is **Bodegas Muga** (*Barrio de Estación. Tel: 941 31 18 25*), which makes some of the most respected reds around. Booking ahead for tours is advised.

Haro's old town is an alluring little place for a wander, with a small ensemble of Baroque and Renaissance structures. At the right time (usually September to March) the distinctive clatter of migrating storks bounces between the rooftops. Take any of the streets leading uphill to the Iglesia de Santo Tómas Apóstol and its richly carved portal of the crucifixion. The streets around it are Haro's *tapeo* stomping ground, a tradition the townsfolk take very seriously indeed. From the early evening onwards, it becomes awash with locals, hopping from one bar to another, class and creed united by the joyous act of eating and drinking.

Laguardia

Cradled by the craggy grey peaks of the Sierra de Cantabria, this captivating hilltop town (Biasteri in the Basque language) has a good number of treasures tucked away behind its ancient walls. Inevitably, it also attracts a sizeable number of tour buses. But in the afternoon, when the setting sun throws a glorious light onto the medieval stone buildings, things quieten down. The whole place is car-free, making it a strollers' delight.

Start your discovery of Laguardia in the Plaza Mayor, and try to do so at noon, 2pm, 5pm or 8pm. At these hours a set of three dancing figures will pop out of the Town Hall's enchanting

La Rioja

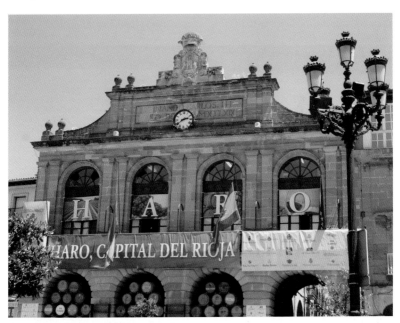

Haro, capital of La Rioja Alta

carillon clock. Then stroll northwards to the **Iglesia de Santa María de los Reyes**. You will need to go inside to see its most stunning feature: a 12th-century, beautifully preserved polychrome portal depicting the apostles (*enquire at the tourist information office in the Plaza San Juan for opening times, which vary. Tel: 945 60 08 45*). Next door is the lofty 13th-century **Torre Abacial**, a defence tower connected to the church via a hanging stone bridge. After this, stroll to the opposite end of the town along the noble Calle Mayor to see the Iglesia de San Juan, a Gothic structure with a fine bell tower.

Laguardia's places of interest are not only at eye level. The town has more than 300 *cuevas* (medieval wineries) lying catacomb-like 6m (20ft) underground. A visit to **El Fabulista** (*see p112*) will give you insight into this centuries-old subterranean activity. As expected, Laguardia is full of great little barrel-lined tapas bars, and its Saturday-morning tapas crawl draws farmers and growers like bees to a honey pot.

The **Museo de Arqueología de Álava** is located in the neighbouring village of La Hoya and has an interesting collection of Bronze and Iron-age objects from the region and the remains of an Iberian settlement on its grounds (*Tel: 945 62 11 22. Open: mid-Oct–end Apr Tue–Sat 11am–3pm, Sun 10am–2pm; rest of the year Tue–Fri 11am–2pm & 4–8pm, Sat 11am–3pm, Sun 10am–2pm. Free admission*).

The dancers on the carillon clock on Plaza Mayor in Laguardia

Logroño

Logroño is every bit the industrious capital city of a prosperous agricultural region. But once you get past the grimy peripheral warehouses, garages and high-rise apartment blocks to the historic centre, you'll find a handful of diamonds in the rough. Foodies take note: along with Seville and San Sebastián, Logroño arguably has one of the most exciting and authentic tapas scenes in the country!

But first the sights. Head south to the old centre, which lies on the banks of the Ebro river. Its centrepiece is the lofty **Santa María la Redonda** with its pair of lovely Baroque bell towers. (Its name comes from the ancient round temple in the cathedral's foundations.) The cathedral sits on the handsome Plaza del Mercado, a buzzing square where regular outdoor markets are held. In contrast, the **Iglesia San Bartolomé** in Plaza San Bartolomé has an interesting Mudéjar (Arabic-Spanish) tower featuring intricate stonework and ceramic tiles. In the Plaza San Agustín you'll find the fanciful neo-Baroque Post Office and Museo de la Rioja (the latter currently closed for renovations).

At night the old town comes alive with Logroño's famous tapas crawl. The centre of action is **Calle Laurel**, which is simply bursting with bars, all packed to the nines after about 9pm. Hop from one to the other, either choosing from trays laden with *pinchos* (the Spanish version of a canapé) or little

Logroño cathedral

earthenware dishes of octopus, bull's tail and other mouth-watering morsels. Recommended are **Pata Negra** (*Number 24*) for the delicious things it does with Iberian ham, and **Bar Angel** (*Number 12*) for wild mushroom *pinchos*.

An exciting new museum is located 9km (5½ miles) away on the outskirts of Logroño. Funded by a German industrialist, the **Museo Würth** contains a wonderful collection of contemporary art (20th–21st-century) and hosts regular temporary exhibitions, concerts and wine-related happenings in a striking modern building (*Polígono Industrial El Sequero, Avenida Los Cameros, Agoncillo. Tel: 941 01 04 10. www.museowurth.es. Open: Mon–Sat 10am–8pm, Sun 10am–3pm. Free admission, and free return shuttle service from the Glorieta del*

The Plaza del Mercado in the centre of Logroño

Dr Zubía in Logroño, Mon, Wed & Fri
6pm, Sat 11.30am & 6pm, Sun 11.30am,
return shuttle leaves the museum two or
two-and-a-half hours later).

San Millán de la Cogolla and monasteries

This tiny village owes its existence to
two of Spain's most renowned – and
visited – monasteries: San Millán de
Suso and San Millán de Yuso. They owe
their name to San Millán (or St
Emilio), a mystic and scribe who
founded a cave-dwelling order of
monks in the 6th century.

Popping out from a wood clearing,
Suso (meaning 'upper'), the older of the
monasteries, is a beautiful pink-hued
sandstone structure built over the
original monks' caves (they are now
rocky-walled chapels), and contains the
tomb of San Millán. But the building's

architectural and historical merits are
overshadowed by its cultural ones. The
Suso monastery developed an important
scriptorium. One codex, the *Glosas
Emilianenses*, is today recognised as the
first written example of the Castilian
language. The document is now kept in
Madrid (though a facsimile and other
illuminated manuscripts written by the
monks are on display in Yuso's treasury),
but this recognition bestowed on Suso
the epithet, 'the Cradle of Castilian',
helping it earn its classification as a
UNESCO World Heritage Site in 1997.

Down below in the valley, the Yuso
(meaning 'lower') monastery dwarfs the
Suso both in terms of size and number
of visitors. Built between the 16th and
18th centuries, it contains an important
sacristy filled with paintings and many
manuscripts written by Suso's scribes,
and an impressive cloister.

Unfortunately, it is also generally overrun by visitors. While not exactly Lourdes, Yuso has developed its own cottage industry: the handful of surrounding shops tout all manner of kitsch, sold by the bucketful to the bus tourists, and part of the monastery has been converted into a hotel. Rather than queuing to go inside, an equally enlightening experience can be had by simply walking through the glorious countryside between Yuso and Suso and admiring the monasteries from the exterior. Follow the path marked 'Ruta de Gonzalo de Barceo' (named after a renowned local poet) from the small cemetery above Yuso.

Tickets for both Yuso and Suso are sold at the Yuso ticket office. They can also be pre-booked or purchased online at *www.monasteriodeyuso.org*

Santo Domingo de la Calzada

A sizeable swathe of La Rioja lies on the pilgrims' route to Santiago de Compostela (*see p41*), and Santo Domingo de la Calzada is one of its most important stopovers. In the 11th century, Domingo (or Dominic) studied in the Monasterio de Valvanera (*see p111*) after which he applied for a residency in the Monasterio de San Millán de la Cogolla (*see opposite*). He wasn't successful, so instead travelled here and set about establishing a hospice (now a *parador, see p149*) for pilgrims on the way to Santiago, and built a bridge for them over the Oja river. Some pilgrims stayed – many too sick to move on and lured by Dominic's reputation as a miracle worker – and a village was born. These days the cathedral, named after the town, is the

La Rioja

The enormous Monasterio de San Millán de Yuso

principal reason the town is perpetually swarming with pilgrims.

Built in 1158 (but with additions in the 14th and 16th centuries), the cathedral dominates the town's central plaza and is a fine medieval ensemble. St Dominic's remains are kept here in the mausoleum, and there is also a Renaissance altar and an intricate Plateresque choir. But its most photographed (and curious) feature is an ornately carved purpose-built cage where white hens are kept. The fowls commemorate the saint's most renowned 'miracle'. As legend has it, a German pilgrim was unjustly accused of theft and sent to be hung. His family continued their journey to Santiago de Compostela, but on the way back found him half-alive on the gallows. They went to the local judge, hoping for a speedy reprieve. The judge was eating his lunch at the time and retorted that the poor sod was no more alive than the bird on his plate, at which point it sat up and clucked. Animal lovers need not be too concerned: the cathedral's hens are rotated regularly from a stock kept at the rear of the pilgrim's hostel to the right of the cathedral.

Cathedral open: Mon–Sat 9.30am–1.30pm & 4–6.30pm.
Admission charge.

A back street leading to the cathedral in Santo Domingo de la Calzada

Sierra de la Demanda

The thrilling Sierra de la Demanda sprawls out over the extreme southwestern corner of La Rioja and into the neighbouring region of Burgos, a region of deep, craggy gorges, verdant valleys blanketed in forests, glacial lakes, ancient stone villages, and with birds of prey gliding over the mountaintops. Known as the 'Rooftop of La Rioja', its highest peak (2,260m/ 7,415ft) is the majestic Mount Urbión, location of the Valdezcaray ski resort. It's more convenient, however, to enter the sierra via the LR113 after visiting the monasteries of San Millán de la Cogolla (*see pp108–9*).

Anguiano is located directly off the highway above the mighty Najerilla river. It's an ancient stone village renowned throughout Spain for its famous and highly bizarre Danza de los Zancos (*see box*). From here on, the scenery gets wilder as you pass through the Roñas Valley, and its birdlife, such as eagles, falcons and partridges, more abundant. Get closer to God (literally) by taking a detour off the highway to visit the **Monasterio de Valvanera**, a Gothic monastery perched high on the peak of San Lorenzo mountain and surrounded by simply breathtaking views. A small chapel contains the wooden statue of the Virgen de Valvanera, La Rioja's patron saint. People flock from all over to pay their respects by lighting candles at her feet (conveniently sold via a slot machine at the entrance to the chapel).

DANZA DE LOS ZANCOS

Anguiano is renowned for its traditional dances, enchanting rituals of swirling white lace skirts, clashing wooden sticks and ribbon formations similar to maypole dancing. But one dance beats them all in terms of sheer strangeness. On the feast of St Magdalene (22 July) and in the last weekend in September, a small group of local youths don skirts and waistcoats and perch themselves on pointed wooden stilts (*zancos*) to perform the Danza de los Zancos. Starting from the entrance to the cathedral (the highest point of the village), they swirl down a steep stone crest in time to music, a hair-raising manoeuvre of dexterity and balance. At the bottom of the hill, the whole village huddles together to form a human 'mattress', ready to cushion the dancers should they fall.

La Rioja

Deeper into the sierra you will find more lost-in-time mountain homesteads. **Canales de la Sierra** is an archetypal village with ancient stone bridges crossing a bubbling stream, and is home to the oldest theatre in Spain and a pair of lovely Romanesque churches. **Mansilla** is more interesting for what it was than what it is now. Pre-1950 it was located at the intersection of two important rivers. When the authorities decided to construct a dam at the location, the townsfolk were moved to a purpose-built village on higher ground. At low tide the rooftops of the old Mansilla peeking up over the water make an eerie sight. **Villavelayo** is also worth going off the highway for – if only for its fanciful Baroque hermitage peppered with child-like sculptures of the saints.

Drive: The emblematic *bodegas* of La Rioja Alavesa

Wine and architecture blend together in La Rioja Alavesa, from centuries-old bodegas *to the new wine palaces designed by the world's über-architects. This pleasant drive through the vineyard-blanketed scenery takes you to some of the most emblematic.*

The drive covers about 50km (31 miles) and could be easily done in a day, taking in the exterior of all the bodegas *mentioned and seeing inside one or two (don't forget to book ahead). Winery tours generally last about an hour. The Marqués de Riscal and Baigorri wineries both have fine restaurants on site (bookings essential).*

Start in Laguardia, right next to the tourist information office.

1 El Fabulista

This ancient subterranean *bodega*, one of many in the extensive network underneath the foundations of the town, is legendary. It once belonged to Félix Samaniego, an illustrious storyteller from Laguardia. Tours include the traditional production facilities (grapes are still pressed by foot) and a tasting at the end (*Plaza San Juan. Tel: 945 62 11 92. www.bodegaelfabulista.com*).
Take the A124 west towards Haro. After a few seconds you will see a sign for
Elvillar/Kripan. Turn right and follow the signs to Ysios.

2 Ysios

Valencian architect Santiago Calatrava's Ysios was the first of the stunning new breed of *bodegas* in La Rioja. Its incredible undulating roof is framed by the backdrop of the Sierra de Cantabria. Inside, the production facilities are no less jaw-dropping, with a tasting room with views over the vines (*Camino de la Hoya. Tel: 945 60 06 40. www.domecqbodegas.com*).
Return to the A124 and turn left towards Logroño. Stop just past Assa.

3 Viña Real

French architect Philippe Mazières has created a minimalist, modernist *bodega* in the shape of a sawn-in-half oak barrel. A skylight bathes the interior in natural light (*Carretera Logroño-Laguardia, Km 4.8. Tel: 945 62 52 55*).
Return on the A124 towards Laguardia. At the intersection of the A3210 turn left and follow the signs for El Ciego.

4 Marqués de Riscal

Frank Gehry's glittering jewel of a hotel for the Marqués de Riscal group is swathed in a spectacular mash of purple, gold and silver titanium ribbons. You'll need a room or restaurant reservation to see inside, though tours are offered of the adjacent *bodega* (*Calle Torrea 1. Tel: 945 18 08 88. www.marquesderiscal.com*). *Return to the A124 via the A3212. Turn left and stop just outside the village of Samaniego.*

5 Baigorri

Baigorri is a specialist breed of winery with a reputation for unique *vinos del autor*. Its *bodega* is a striking glass 'box' jutting out from the crest of a hill. The high-tech production facilities are underground (*Carretera Vitoria-*

Logroño, Km 53. Tel: 945 60 94 20. www.bodegasbaigorri.com).
Continue on the A124, following the signs for Vitoria. At Briñas take the N124 towards Haro. On approach, follow the signs to the Barrio de Estación.

6 Viña Tondonia

Viña Tondonia is the oldest of Haro's *bodegas*. The tour of their facilities takes in the seemingly endless miles of underground tunnels and a fabulously quirky, decanter-shaped extension by architect Zaha Hadid (*Avenida de Vizcaya 3. Tel: 941 31 02 44. www.lopezdeheredia.com).*
If you have time on the way back to Laguardia, visit the fabulous Wine Museum in Briones (see p99), signposted off the N124.

Drive: The emblematic *bodegas* of La Rioja Alavesa

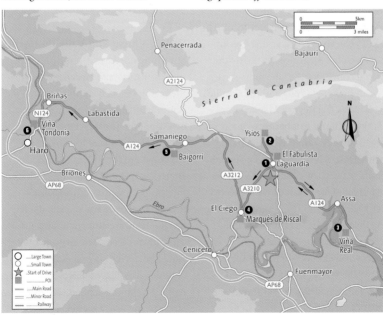

The Aragonese Pyrenees

The Aragonese (or Eastern) Pyrenees may not be as well known as their Catalan counterparts. But those with the wanderlust to venture to the extreme north of Spain's largest region will be well rewarded. Monasteries and castles cling impossibly to dramatic cliffs, deep gorges are cut through the mountains, and medieval villages are seemingly lost in time. For nature and outdoor sport enthusiasts, it offers plenty of opportunities, from scaling a 300m-high (980ft) rock to birdwatching.

Out of all the regions covered in this book, Northern Aragón certainly feels the most remote and oblivious to the modern world. The majority of the destinations in this chapter largely fall within the Jacetainia sub-region (or *comarca*) where the 'high valleys' and mountains bordering France are at their most breathtakingly beautiful. The pre-Pyrenean south, guarded over by the awesome Mallos rocks, boasts the architectural jewels of the monasteries of San Juan de la Peña and the Castillo de Loarre. The mighty Aragón river marks a natural frontier between northern and southern Jacetainia, whose path has forged majestic gorges and a network of canals, and provides a playground for a host of water-related activities such as rafting and canyoning. Further west, the Parque Natural de Ordesa hosts some of the most spectacular hiking country in Spain.

Northern Aragón is a slow-paced region. Even during the ski season, the city of Jaca feels like it's stuck in first gear. Arrive at a remote mountain village in the mid-afternoon and the only company you may have is likely to be the majestic birds of prey that perpetually circle the peaks. For lovers of nature, landscape and solitude, a holiday doesn't come much better than this.

Valle de Ansó and Valle de Hecho

Stretching northeast from Jaca, the valleys of Ansó and Hecho are two of the region's most beautiful. Isolated for centuries, the people here speak their own language (called Cheso) and their ancient stone villages have made little concession to the modern world. The scenery is splendid, with gorges, thick forests and streams – it's a walker's dream. The roads, bar the inevitable hairpin turn, are also good for touring. The only problems you may encounter would be during snow season.

Both valleys have villages of the same name. **Hecho** (or Echo in Cheso) is the larger of the two, a picture-perfect little ensemble of immaculately kept whitewashed mountain homes with pretty geranium-filled flower gardens and slate roofs. Eagles and other birds of prey fly between the rooftops, and on the outskirts there is an unusual modern sculpture garden – a legacy from a past culturefest. Food lovers should pre-book a table at the wonderful **Restaurante Gaby**, which serves up the best home-cooking in the valley (*Tel: 974 37 50 07*).

North of Hecho lies the **Selva de Oza**, a wonderful forest of giant oak and pine trees and thick ferns. At its entrance you'll come across the **Boca del Infierno** ('Hell's Mouth'), an impressive gorge and a hunting ground for wallcreepers, a pretty red and white

mountain bird that feeds off insects in the rocks. Also close by is the tiny hamlet of **Siresa**, dominated by a bulky Romanesque monastery, a stopover on the Aragonese-Santiago route.

Ansó, in the neighbouring valley, offers more of the same charm and character. The village is famous for preserving its language and culture and on the last Sunday of every August the townsfolk dress in traditional costume, a spectacle that draws crowds from all over. At other times, you can see the traditional clothing and artefacts of these valleys at the tiny **Museo del Traje Ansotano**, located above the church (*Open: summer only, or enquire at the Town Hall on the main square*).

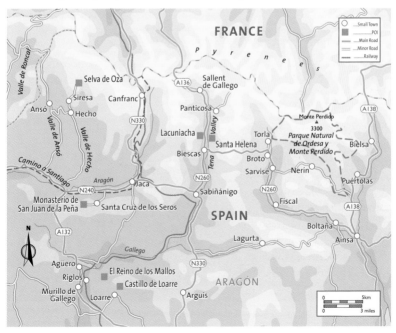

Castillo de Loarre

If it's castles in Spain you have come to see, look no further. The Castillo de Loarre is not only the best in Northern Spain, but also possibly the whole country. All the elements are here: a hair-raising mountaintop setting with panoramic views over the endless plains below, secret walkways, a knight's chapel, towers, battlements and dungeons – all that's missing are the dragons.

Dating from the 11th century and one of the few secular structures to survive from the Romanesque period, it was built on the site of an earlier Roman fort before it became a castle under the dynasties of the first Kings of Aragón, and later a monastery. Perched 1,000m (3,280ft) above ground on the peak of a craggy mountain, it almost morphs into its natural setting, making it difficult from a distance to decipher rock from wall. One if its most outstanding features is the crypt of the Iglesia de San Pedro at the entrance, a breathtakingly serene, domed-shape space surrounded by delicate, arched marble windows. The rest of the castle is a myriad of pavilions, ramps, chambers and look-out towers once used to keep watch on approaching Muslim invaders. Don't miss the Mirador de la Reina which, on a clear day, will allow you sweeping views of the entire Ebro Valley.
Tel: 974 34 21 61.
www.castillodeloare.com.
Open: mid-Jun–mid-Sept 10am–2pm & 4–7pm; mid-Oct–mid-Jun slightly reduced hours. Admission charge.

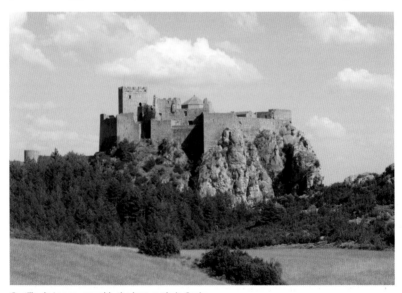

Castillo de Loarre, arguably the best castle in Spain

Jaca

The main city and gateway to the Aragonese Pyrenees, Jaca is a slightly puzzling place. The stunning mountain backdrop aside, at first glance it looks like a generic modern city, with roundabouts, supermarkets and dozens of nondescript hotels, none of which gives a hint of the town's important place in history (it was the first capital of the Kingdom of Aragón). But make your way from the wide Avenida de Primer Viernes de Mayo and you will come across Jaca's small and compact ancient heart, all the more remarkable for the fact that, amid the modern build-up, it's simply there.

The city's cathedral **San Pedro el Viejo** was the first in the country to be built in the Romanesque style, though its interior dates from later periods (*Open: 11.30am–1.30pm & 4.30–7pm. Free admission*). It's a gem – but like the rest of Jaca, a curious one – and seemingly melts into its medieval neighbours without making a noise. Its most beguiling features are its portals: the main entrance is richly carved with beasts and a *crimsón*, the ancient symbol of Christ and infinity. The southern door has a finely constructed porch from a later era and beautifully carved capitals, attributed to the mysterious 'Maestro'. Inside, the interior's most outstanding features are its cloisters, home to the Museo Diocesano, which contains one of the most renowned collections of

THE END OF THE LINE

Trainspotters and history curio enthusiasts will find Canfranc an interesting detour. Located north of Jaca a few kilometres from the French border, the village was almost completely destroyed by a dreadful fire in 1944. It has now been entirely rebuilt, an outcome many wish on the Canfranc-Estación. When it opened in 1928, this beautiful railway station became a symbol of connection to Europe for Aragón's isolated village communities and was used as a location in the film *Dr Zhivago*. But the line from France was closed off in 1970s, leaving it to the elements. A few trains a day still chug in from Zaragoza, but for the most part Canfranc-Estación remains a glorious relic of another age.

Romanesque art in Spain (*currently closed for renovations, but due to reopen in early 2010*). The streets in the immediate vicinity of the cathedral are full of cobblestoned charm, with some wonderful tapas bars and gourmet shops selling local wine and foodstuffs.

You'll need to cross over the Avenida de Primer Viernes de Mayo again to see Jaca's other main sight: the vast **Cuitadella** (*Tel: 974 36 37 46. Open: Tue–Sun 11am–2pm & 5–8pm. Admission charge*). This pentagon-shaped fortress was built during the reign of Felipe II in the 16th century to keep out the French, and it's still in use by Spain's military. You can see it if you are willing to pay the rather lofty admission charge, which also gives access to a museum containing 35,000 miniature lead soldiers.

Monasterio de San Juan de la Peña

The thrilling monasteries of San Juan de la Peña are located on the high ground of the pre-Pyrenees, a simply outstanding location blanketed in thick forests and with the snow-capped mountains of the Pyrenees proper providing a breathtaking backdrop. Getting there via the snaking mountain road is half the thrill and the Monasterio Nuevo (New Monastery) has plenty of picnic and parking facilities in its grounds, so pack a lunch.

The New Monastery, the starting point of the visit, is an impressive early 17th-century structure built after a fire destroyed the Old (or Royal) Monastery that lies a kilometre down the mountain. It has a rich Baroque entrance and two fine bell towers, though a renovation in 2005 has lent the building an air of pastiche. Inside, there is a hotel and space for exhibitions, though only a fraction of the interior is open to the general public

Eschew the shuttle bus and instead take a stroll through the forest (follow the path from the information office to the left of the New Monastery) to San Juan de la Peña, the original. It was founded in the 10th century by a group of hermit-monks, who were supposedly searching for a hiding place for the Holy Grail. They couldn't have chosen a better place; this heart-stopping structure has been nestled into the side of an overhanging wall of the mountain (*peña* means 'cliff' or 'rock face'). No

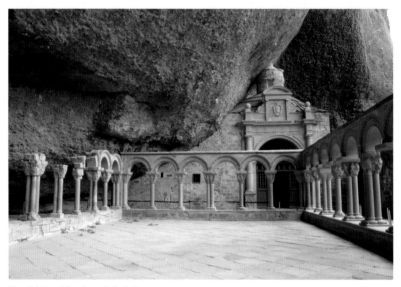

The cloister at San Juan de la Peña

The original monastery looks as though it was carved out of the rock

real grail is to be found inside today, but there are plenty of settings fit for a Dan Brown novel. The subterranean chambers – the oldest part of the monastery – have vestiges of Romanesque murals. The 12th-century necropolis contains the tombs of some of the early Kings of Aragón, exquisitely carved in creamy-white alabaster. This neoclassical Royal Pantheon has some rich stuccowork on its walls, with scenes from Aragón's early history and a replica of the grail in the chapel. But it's the cloister that will take your breath away – 25 Romanesque columns demark the area, each with a capital delicately carved with doe-eyed figurines depicting scenes from the Bible in chronological order. Like Jaca's

cathedral, this work is simply attributed to 'El Maestro'. Like all outstanding Romanesque decorative work in the Pyrenees, it is highly graphic, clearly conceived to convey the scriptures to the illiterate masses.

The final part of the visit takes you though a splendid Mozarabic portal to the Gothic chapel, resting place of the abbots and the section of the monastery where its rocky walls are most evident. *Tel: 974 35 51 19.*
www.monasteriosanjuan.com. Open: Nov–mid-Mar 11am–2pm & 3.30–6pm; mid-Mar–end May 10am–2pm & 3.30–7pm; Jun–mid-Jul 10am–2pm & 3–8pm; mid-Jul–end Aug 10am–8pm; Sept–Oct 10am–2pm & 3.30–7pm. Admission charge.

El Reino de los Mallos

Reino (or Kingdom) may seem like an odd name to denote a swathe of landscape dominated by rock formations. But unless you have seen Australia's Uluru or Gibraltar, chances are you have never experienced rocks quite like the phenomenal Mallos. These nine russet-red towers of rock reach a height of 300m (984ft), guarding the ground below like giant centurions. They are considered some of the best rock-climbing territory in Spain, and on any given day you'll see handfuls of brave souls on them, armed with ropes and axes. For most of us, admiring their majesties from ground level is enough.

The Mallos rise up from the Gallego river

There are several villages in the area where you can do this. **Riglos** is the most popular, with a bar-restaurant that has an outdoor terrace for viewing the rocks and the eagles and vultures that swoop effortlessly over them. It is also close enough for you to walk from here up to their gigantic base. **Agüero** is a tiny hamlet dominated by the overhanging Peña Sola, with a notable Romanesque church attributed to the architect of San Juan de la Peña. **Murillo de Gallego** is located on the river of the same name. Its Romanesque church sits high up against the backdrop of Los Mallos, and has a good *bodega* where you can try local wine (*see box*).

The odd-shaped chimneys stand out as you look around Santa Cruz de los Seros

Santa Cruz de los Seros

Cradled in a valley on the descent from San Juan de la Peña (*see pp118–19*) to Jaca, this lovely little village is seemingly devoid of a single concession to the modern world. The handful of homesteads bears the trademark characteristics of Aragonese mountain architecture: thick-stone brick walls, and pointed slate roofs with curious cylindrical chimneys called *espantabrujas* ('witch-scarers'). Some of them have been turned into restaurants serving up healthy portions of mountain food, making this a good stop for lunch. There are also a couple of enticing ceramic shops in the main square.

The village is also renowned for its two beautiful examples of Romanesque churches. The first, at the entrance to the village and alone on a green field, is the tiny, single-nave, Lombard-style Iglesia de San Caprasio, which functioned as the parish church until the nuns abandoned it in 1555. There is a grid over its front door, which is usually open to let you see its (restored) whitewashed interior and altar. The second church, in the main square, is the Iglesia de Santa María, with a four-tiered mullioned tower and impressive portal denoting a *crimsón* and lions – similar to that of the cathedral in Jaca (*see p117*).

Valle de Tena

Though not as spectacular as those of Ansó and Hecho (*see pp114–15*), the Tena Valley is popular with skiers and hikers and has good facilities. If you are travelling with kids, they will have a fine day out at **Lacuniacha**, a 'fauna park' that lets them get up close and personal with all sorts of cuddly creatures (*www.lacuniacha.com*). If you are lucky, you may even see the rare Iberian lynx.

Biescas and its immediate surroundings is one of the valley's highlights. It's a fine Pyrenean village

The Embalse de Bubal reservoir in the Tena Valley

divided in two by the rushing Gallego river. Each side has its own church: the San Pedro and the San Salvador. Also worth seeking out to the north is the **hermitage and dolmen of Santa Helena** on the A136 towards France. After a few kilometres the highway will cross the river. Leave the car at the side of the road and cross the bridge (there are signposts). Take the right-leading track through the thick forest to the dolmens, well-preserved funerary monuments from the Bronze Age. The left track will take you along the riverbank to the abandoned village of Polituara, the location of the hermitage that is dedicated to the patron saint of the valley. It was built under the reign of Jaime I in the 8th century and has been fairly poorly restored, though its lovely isolated setting is worth the effort.

Further northward into the valley, the village of **Panticosa** is located near a beautiful gorge of the same name and is the base for the Panticosa ski resorts. It is also home to a famous spa-hotel (*www.panticosa.com*) which has been popular with the Spanish elite since the 19th century. An annexe has just been added by the Pritzker-Prize-winning architect Rafael Moneo.

Near the border of France, **Sallent de Gallego** is the valley's largest town. Located on the edge of the Lanuza dam, its population swells in winter (with skiers using the nearby station Formigal) and in summer when it plays host to the popular Pirineos Sur world music festival (*www.pirineos-sur.es*).

Biescas is a must-see in the Tena Valley

Parque Natural de Ordesa y Monte Perdido (Ordesa Natural Park and Lost Mountain)

Undoubtedly the feather in the Western Pyrenees' cap is Ordesa Natural Park. Covering more than 15,000 hectares (37,000 acres), the Ordesa Valley was created by a glacier that sliced through a limestone massif, leaving in its wake some of the most jaw-dropping scenery in Spain.

Declared a protected area in 1928, Ordesa is blessed with high escarpments, deep canyons and thick forests of beech, fir and black pine. At its northern tip, Monte Perdido

Ordesa Natural Park

('Lost Mountain') looms 3,300m (10,820ft) high over the valley. Ordesa's abundant birdlife, wild horses, the odd deer, marmot and *jabalí* (wild boar) make it a nature lover's dream. But you'll need your hiking boots; most of the park is only accessible on foot.

Most people leave their car at the string of villages around the ring of the park. Lovely **Torla**, on the western edge of Ordesa, is the most convenient. It has an **information office** (*Tel: 974 48 63 78. Open: Easter Week & Jun–end Oct Mon–Sat 9.30am–1.30pm & 5–9pm*) and a shuttle bus service (every 15 minutes) to the entrance of the park. It also has a good choice of accommodation, restaurants and adventure-sports providers. Slightly further south, **Broto** and **Sarvisé**, with a handful of *casas rurales* (rural homesteads) and other services, are also options, though you will need your own transport.

One of the most popular hikes (five or six hours return) starts from the car park, located 8km (5 miles) from Torla. (From June until the end of September you will need to take the

Cliffs dominate the surroundings of Torla

shuttle bus from the village; the rest of the year you can drive your car directly there.) Follow the riverside path up to the Cola de Caballo, a stunning waterfall that drops from various natural terraces high up in the valley. Along the way you will pass through the thick oak forest of the Bosque de los Faus, caves, a glacial cirque and open fields which afford a wonderful view of Monte Perdido.

Another shorter, easier option is directly from Torla village itself, following the 'Sendero de Turieta'. Take the stone bridge over the Azaras river and follow it past some wonderful waterfalls and through a fir forest to the Pradera de Ordesa, the location of the car park. From here you can take the shuttle bus back to Torla. Whatever the weather and route you choose, make sure you are prepared. Pick up a detailed map of the park before you set off, and keep in mind that sudden changes in temperature can occur.

For those who don't want to leave the comfort of their car, there is a winding forest road that leads from Sarvisé to **Nerín**, a tiny hamlet at an altitude of 2,200m (7,220ft). There are simply stunning valley views from the various *miradors* along the way.

Ainsa on the park's southernmost tip is a destination within itself, prestigiously situated on the confluence of two rivers and with a dramatic mountain backdrop. It boasts a near-perfect ensemble of 12th-century architecture spanning out from the arcaded main square. Climb the tower of the Romanesque church for a view over the village's enchanting rooftops.

The Catalan Pyrenees

The remote mountain valleys of the Eastern Pyrenees are the heartland of Catalunya, a beautiful region with a long history, which remains proud of its distinct language, culture and traditions. The superb regional cuisine, world-class Romanesque architecture and breathtaking mountain scenery are the main attractions here, and it's a paradise for all kinds of outdoor activities, from skiing to climbing. Best of all, thanks to the proximity of the Mediterranean, year-round sunshine is almost guaranteed.

Catalunya emerged in the early Middle Ages from the Spanish Marches, a buffer zone between the Frankish Empire to the north of the Pyrenees and the Muslim kingdom of Al-Andalus to the south. The counts of these mountain valleys were appointed by the Franks, but from the 9th century gradually assumed increasing independence. The founding father of nascent Catalunya was Guifré El Pilós (Wilfred the Hairy), whose exploits gained him almost mythical status. He was responsible for the founding of the great monastery at Ripoll, which was later endowed with its spectacular portal, among the finest Romanesque artworks to be found anywhere in Europe. Gradually, from the 11th to the 13th centuries, the mountains filled up with exquisite Romanesque churches, built on the northern Italian (Lombard) model, with lofty, slender bell towers and lavish fresco decoration. These are now recognised by UNESCO for their outstanding beauty. They are set amid spectacular mountain scenery, which reaches its apotheosis in the Parc Nacional d'Aigüestortes i Estany de Sant Maurici, a natural wonderland of craggy peaks, lakes, rivers and waterfalls. Spain's best ski resorts are concentrated in these lofty Pyrenean valleys and in the tiny Principality of Andorra which borders Catalunya.

Andorra

The Principat d'Andorra (Principality of Andorra) is one of the highest and smallest countries in Europe, nestled between France and Spain in the Eastern Pyrenees. According to legend, Andorra was founded by Emperor Charlemagne in 805 in gratitude for local support in the wars against the Saracens. Later, the region was co-ruled by the Bishop of Urgell and the Count of Foix (a title later acquired by the French king), and this pact was confirmed in a treaty signed in 1278. This treaty was important because it established Andorra's political and territorial borders. Officially, Andorra is still a co-principality, with the President of France (as successor to the French king) and the Bishop of Urgell as co-princes – a symbolic tribute, which includes a few hams, cheeses and chickens, is paid annually. In practice, however, Andorra is an independent parliamentary democracy.

Until the 1940s it was poor and almost completely isolated, but it has developed as a major tourist destination in the last decades thanks to the growing popularity of skiing. More recently, its tax-free status has brought in hordes of visitors hoping to stock up on duty-free goods. However, development has taken its toll, and parts of Andorra's once-pristine landscape have been disfigured by shopping malls and hastily built resorts. But it's still possible to find some hidden corners of heart-stopping beauty which the developers have yet to exploit.

Andorra La Vella

Andorra La Vella is the capital of Andorra, a brash, modern city surrounded by lofty Pyrenean peaks. Most people come for the shopping, but it does have a small Barri Antic (Old Quarter) with a couple of charming Romanesque churches and the Casa de la Vall, a 16th-century mansion that now houses the Andorran parliament. Just outside Andorra La Vella, the Romanesque church of Sant Miquel, with its slender bell tower,

The Catalan Pyrenees

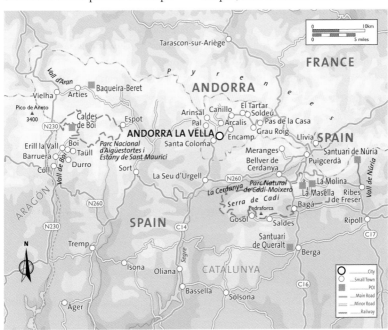

overlooks the tranquil lake Estany d'Engolasters, set in meadows. It's a good starting point for several wonderful hikes.

Romanesque churches

Andorra has preserved more than 40 fine Romanesque churches, notably in the little village of Pal, which is one of the loveliest and least spoilt in all Andorra. The **Andorra Romànica Centre d'Interpretació** (Andorran Romanesque Interpretation Centre) provides an introduction to the style, and exhibits some exquisite Romanesque artworks (*Carrer Sant Climent, Pal. Tel: (+376) 83 69 08. Open: Tue–Sat 9.30am–1.30pm & 3–6.30pm, Sun 10am–2pm. Free admission*). Other superb churches include Sant Joan de Caselles, on the outskirts of Canillo, and Santa Coloma, on the southern fringes of Andorra la Vella. Santa Coloma dates from the 9th century and is one of the oldest churches in Andorra.

Skiing and outdoor activities

Andorra has combined all its ski resorts into two massive complexes: **Grandvalira** (*www.grandvalira.com*) and **Vallnord** (*www.vallnord.com*). Grandvalira is the largest, with 193km (120 miles) of pistes, and encompasses the ski centres of Pas de la Casa, Grau Roig, Soldeu, El Tartar, Canillo and Encamp. Vallnord includes Arcalís, Arinsal and Pal. They are equipped with every modern amenity and offer an enormous variety of winter sports, including downhill, off-piste and cross-country skiing, snowboarding, paragliding, adventure activities, motocross and dog-sledding. Other popular outdoor activities include hiking, rock climbing and mountaineering, mountain biking, fishing and adventure sports such as

Estany d'Engolasters in Andorra

whitewater rafting. The Andorran **tourist information office** (*www.andorra.ad*) can provide comprehensive information on the activities offered.

La Cerdanya

La Cerdanya is a vast, green Pyrenean valley, fertile and well watered by the Segre river. Despite the altitude, which averages around 1,000m (3,280ft), it is usually warm and sunny, and is sheltered to the north by the Pyrenees and to the south by the Cadí and Moixeró mountain ranges. In the 8th century, the county of Cerdanya was incorporated into the Spanish Marches, a buffer zone between Christian and Muslim territories established by Emperor Charlemagne. The Cerdanya's strategic location on important trade routes ensured its increasing power and influence, particularly during the 11th and 12th centuries. The ancient capital of the Cerdanya was Llívia (*see p131*), but the capital was transferred to Puigcerdà (*see p135*) in the 12th century. In 1659, the northern half of the Cerdanya Valley was ceded to France under the Treaty of the Pyrenees. Even now, however, the two halves of the valley continue to maintain strong ties, and Catalan, rather than French or Spanish, is still the lingua franca.

Like other Eastern Pyrenean valleys, the Cerdanya is well endowed with Romanesque architecture. The **tourist information office** (*www.cerdanya.org*)

THE CATALAN LANGUAGE

There are three official languages in Catalunya: Castillian Spanish, Catalan and Aranese. Catalan, a Romance language which began to develop in the early Middle Ages, is most widely spoken, particularly in the Pyrenean region. It has been systematically repressed throughout several dark periods in Catalunya's history, most recently by the dictator General Franco, but is currently being vigorously promulgated by the Catalan government. More people speak Catalan as their mother tongue than Danish, and a campaign is currently underway to have it recognised as an official language by the European Union.

publishes a series of pamphlets outlining special routes through the valley which highlight some of the finest churches. There's a particularly lovely group in the Meranges Valley, one of the most remote corners of the Cerdanya. Most of the Cerdanya's villages have retained their old-fashioned, rural appeal, and many offer wonderful country accommodation in *cases rurales*. Try to catch a weekly market, where you may be able to pick up local delicacies such as handmade cheeses, honey and *botifarra* (Catalan sausages).

The Cerdanya has become a very popular destination for outdoor activities, particularly hiking, mountain biking, rock climbing, fishing, golf and a wide range of winter sports including skiing and snowboarding (the biggest resorts are La Molina and La Masella). It is one of the gateways to the extensive Parc Natural de Cadí-Moixeró (*see pp136–7*).

La Seu d'Urgell

The historic seat of the powerful Bishopric of Urgell, the little city of La Seu d'Urgell sits at the confluence of the rivers Segre and Valira and overlooks a small plain. The Bishop of Urgell is still one of the nominal co-princes of Andorra (*see pp126–9*), just 9km (5½ miles) to the north, but the city has long lost its medieval importance. However, it has managed to retain its spectacular Romanesque cathedral, the finest in Catalunya, and a clutch of atmospheric old streets in the Casc Antic (Old Town).

Casc Antic (Old Town)

The finest street of medieval La Seu d'Urgell was Carrer dels Canonges, which means 'Street of the Clerics'. The street, still handsomely lined with porticos, frames, at its farthest end, the main façade of the cathedral. The **Catedral de Santa Maria** is one of the oldest and best-preserved Romanesque cathedrals in Spain, established in the 9th century but twice rebuilt. This is the third church to occupy the site and was begun in 1116. Inside, it is austere and contemplative, with a soaring nave dimly lit by narrow windows. The highlight is the exquisite cloister, with its wonderful, early Romanesque carved capitals featuring an entire menagerie of fabulous creatures. Just off the cloister is the little church of **Sant Miquel**, a miniature jewel of early medieval architecture, and the only part of the previous cathedral complex still standing.

The Romanesque Catedral de Santa María in La Seu d'Urgell

Other sights

On the edge of La Seu d'Urgell, the leafy Vallira park on the banks of the river contains an interesting curiosity. The **Cloister of Racionera** is a copy of the cathedral cloister but, instead of medieval creatures, the capitals are carved with famous faces, from Sophia Loren to Picasso. Also on the outskirts of La Seu d'Urgell, the village of **Castellciutat** was once crowned by a castle belonging to the Counts of Urgell. The remnants of the castle have been converted into a smart hotel.

Watersports and other activities

La Seu d'Urgell was briefly in the international spotlight in 1992, when Barcelona hosted the Olympic Games and this Pyrenean city was chosen to host some of the watersport events. The Parc Olímpic del Segre is still functioning as a sports venue, with excellent facilities for canoeing, rafting, kayaking or, for the less ambitious, enjoyable boat rides. The Organyà gorge, just south of town, is a mecca for adventure sports including hang-gliding.

Llívia

Llívia is an historical curiosity. This modest little country town, population 1,400, is a Spanish exclave – a Spanish possession entirely surrounded by French territory. This strange state of affairs came about in 1659 when, under the Treaty of the Pyrenees, Spain ceded the northern swathe of the Cerdanya

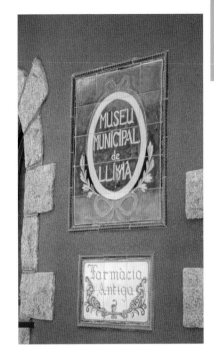

Europe's oldest pharmacy

Valley to the French. The treaty specified that the villages of the northern Cerdanya would go to France, but Llívia, which was the ancient capital of the valley and therefore was classified as a town, declared itself exempt and remained Spanish.

Llívia has one other claim to fame: Europe's oldest pharmacy, which was in operation from 1594 to 1926, has been carefully moved to the town's municipal museum (currently being remodelled). Tourism has become increasingly important in recent years, and the surrounding area offers plenty of opportunities for walking, biking and mountain sports.

Catalan Romanesque art and architecture

From the 10th to the 12th centuries, in the newly emerging nation of Catalunya (and parts of the Aragonese Pyrenees), churches and monasteries were being built by stonemasons, master painters, sculptors and artisans from northern Italy and southern France. These outstanding artists introduced Romanesque architecture (the first distinctive architectural style to spread across Europe since the collapse of the Roman Empire) to the region. It would develop its own distinctive characteristics, which drew on influences not just from north of the Pyrenees, but also from the Visigoths who had formerly ruled much of the Iberian Peninsula, and the Mozarabic miniaturists. The style reached its apogee in the Vall de Boí (Boí Valley, see pp138–9), which still contains the greatest concentration of Romanesque art anywhere in Europe, and has been recognised by UNESCO.

Virtually every village in the Vall de Boí, a narrow, steep-sided valley high in the Pyrenees, still boasts a graceful Romanesque church. The Lombard influence is clearly apparent, most notably in the tall, slim bell towers with their mullioned windows. The bell towers also functioned as watchtowers, necessary in those war-torn times, and some had as many as six storeys. The churches were built on a cross plan, with either one or three naves, and were richly decorated inside with magnificent frescoes. These spellbinding frescoes depicted Biblical stories, mythical creatures and stylised figures, such as the huge Christ Pantocrater ('Christ in Majesty', an important and recurrent image in Romanesque art) which dominates the apse of the sublime church of

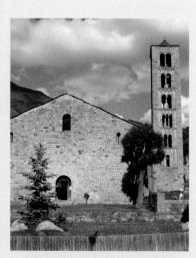

Santa Maria church in Taüll

Sant Climent in Taüll. Most of the original frescoes have been moved to the Museu Nacional d'Art de Catalunya (National Art Museum of Catalunya) in Barcelona, and have been replaced with reproductions. These only hint at how the churches might have looked 800 or 900 years ago, when the colours were vivid and the frescoes were lit only by flickering candles. The images covered every inch of the walls and columns, the lavish decoration not simply a homage to God, but also a visual lesson to the largely illiterate congregation – a reminder of the punishments that awaited those who didn't remain true to the Christian faith. For these churches stood on the front line of the battle between the Christian kingdoms of the north and the vast Muslim caliphate of Al-Andalus which lay to the south. Other outstanding churches in the same valley include Santa Maria (Taüll), Sant Joan (Boí), Santa Eulàlia (Erill la Vall), Sant Feliu (Barruera), the Nativitat (Durro), Santa Maria (Cóll) and the little hermitage of Sant Quirc just outside Durro.

The other great Romanesque monument in Catalunya is the superb portal at the Monestir de Santa Maria in Ripoll (see p136). This, along with the adjacent cloister, is virtually all that survives of the original 11th–14th-century monastery, one of the most

Inside the Nativitat in Durro

important religious institutions in medieval Catalunya. The magnificent portal is thickly decorated with numerous scenes from the Bible, while the cloister is celebrated for its exquisitely sculpted columns.

Almost as fine is the cathedral in La Seu d'Urgell (see p130), the best surviving Romanesque cathedral in all Spain. Humbler (yet still breathtakingly lovely) Romanesque churches are liberally sprinkled throughout the rural villages of the high Pyrenees, both in Catalunya and across the border in Andorra. Many still contain traces of their original frescoes, and stand testament to the gifted artists – almost all anonymous – whose works have survived for almost a thousand years.

Parc Nacional d'Aigüestortes i Estany de Sant Maurici (National Park of Aigüestortes and the Lake of St Maurice)

High in the Pyrenees, the Parc Nacional d'Aigüestortes encompasses snow-capped peaks, rushing streams, waterfalls and vast glacial lakes. It is spectacularly beautiful and miraculously unspoilt, and the presence of so much water (*aigüestortes* means 'twisted waters' in Catalan) gives it a very special allure. Come in late spring to enjoy meadows full of wild flowers and rivers in full spate.

Access

Access is carefully regulated and vehicles are strictly forbidden. The two main entry points are Boí, to the east, and Espot, to the west. The park information offices in each of these towns can provide maps showing some of the easier walking routes, and offer an overview of the park's flora and fauna. They also provide a jeep service (for a fee) to the Estany de Sant Maurici, one of the park's most famous sights and the starting point for some fantastic walking trails. In summer, information kiosks can be found at the car parks and in some of the park's most popular locations.

Flora and fauna

A number of ecosystems are found within the park boundaries, supporting a very wide variety of flora and fauna. Of the numerous bird species to be found here, some of the most commonly seen are the capercaillie, ptarmigan, griffon vulture and the Lammergeier (known in Catalan as the *trencalòs*, which means 'bone-breaker'). Animals include chamois, fox, otter, stoat and the very elusive brown bear (almost extinct, although Slovenian bears have recently been introduced).

Hiking and camping

The GR11, the famous trans-Pyrenean long-distance walking path, crosses the entire breadth of the park and is the most famous of many hiking trails. The range of walking paths means that there is something suitable for walkers of all abilities. Long-distance walkers can make use of ten mountain *refugis*, or shelters (usually open in spring and summer, and for limited periods at Christmas and Easter), as camping is prohibited.

A waterfall in Parc Nacional d'Aigüestortes

Artificial lake at Puigcerdà, built in the 1200s

Puigcerdà

Capital of the Cerdanya since the 12th century, Puigcerdà is a lively little mountain town located just a couple of kilometres from the French-Spanish border. From the end of the 19th century, it became a popular summer retreat for well-heeled Barcelonians, and it still boasts a sprinkling of pretty turn-of-the-20th-century summer villas on its outskirts. Puigcerdà lost most of its historic monuments during the Spanish Civil War (1936–9), but the cool mountain air and the proximity of several ski resorts still attract affluent visitors from either side of the border throughout the year.

The main appeal of the old town centre lies in its colourful little squares, with their terrace cafés and markets, and the narrow streets lined with smart boutiques. A bell tower is all that has survived of the 12th-century church of Santa Maria in the heart of town. Another church, the 13th-century **Església de Sant Domènec**, fared a little better, and contains faded remnants of Romanesque frescoes (*Passeig 10 Abril. Tel: 972 88 04 62. Open: 9am–1pm & 4–8.30pm. Free admission*).

But Puigcerdà's biggest attraction is undoubtedly the huge lake on the edge of town. The *estany* (or lake) was created in the 13th century and has been a favourite place for leisure and relaxation ever since. The rowing events of the 1992 Olympic Games took place here, when the public park that surrounds the lake was expanded and provided with excellent facilities for watersports.

Ripoll

Ripoll is now a quiet country town, ringed with forested peaks, which has frankly seen better days. It's hard to believe that it was from here that the Catalan nation emerged, under the rule of Guifré El Pilós (Wilfred the Hairy), who united several counties in the Eastern Pyrenees and consolidated his power by establishing churches and monasteries. One of the earliest and most prestigious was the **Monestir de Santa Maria** in Ripoll (*Plaça del Monestir. Tel: 972 70 42 03. Open: Oct–Mar 10am–1pm & 3–6pm; Apr–Sept 10am–1pm & 3–7pm. Admission charge*). It would become an important centre of learning, with a famous Scriptorium, as well as the pantheon for Guifré's descendants, the Counts of Barcelona. Unfortunately, the monastery was badly shaken by an earthquake in the 15th century and virtually destroyed by Napoleon's armies in the early 1800s. Almost miraculously, the main portal and the cloister survive. These constitute two of the finest works of Romanesque art anywhere in the world.

The portal has been described as 'a Bible in stone' and is utterly breathtaking. The doorway is thickly covered with hundreds of intricately carved Biblical scenes, from Daniel in the Lion's Den to Jonah and the Whale. Secular themes are also present, including symbols of the zodiac, and the utterly enchanting Labours of the Months, which beautifully depict the

THE LEGEND OF THE CATALAN FLAG

The 9th-century Count Guifré El Pilós (Wilfred the Hairy) is considered the forefather of the Catalan nation. Of the many myths and legends which have been attributed to him, the most famous is the creation of the Catalan *Senyera* (flag). According to legend, the count's overlord, the Frankish King Carles El Calb (Charles the Bald), saw Wilfred dying on the battlefield in 897. The king dipped his fingers in Wilfred's blood and drew them down his golden shield. The four scarlet stripes against a golden background have been Catalunya's standard ever since.

tasks – picking the grapes, killing the pig – demanded throughout the year. The church was destroyed by the French armies and unsympathetically restored in the late 19th century. The nave is still lined with the sarcophagi of the Counts of Barcelona and there is a memorial to Guifré El Pilós, whose bones were lost in the destruction. The enchanting double-storey cloister is framed with graceful columns, each with intricate sculptural decoration. Only the north wing is original; the rest of the cloister is a 19th-century neo-Gothic reconstruction.

Serra de Cadí

The Serra de Cadí is a huge, pre-Pyrenean mountain range which is a very popular destination for hikers and mountain climbers. It, along with the adjoining Moixeró mountains, is a protected nature reserve, the Parc Natural de Cadí-Moixeró. There is a park information office in the sleepy little town of **Bagá**, set in picturesque hills (take the tiny back roads to admire the spectacular scenery).

The main town in this region is **Berga**, an otherwise quiet market town that explodes on the feast of Corpus Christi (May or June) with an anarchic festival called La Patum, which features fireworks, dragons, demons and a terrifying dance by masked figures. Berga, like Bagá, is a good walking base, and one of its most popular excursions is the hour-long hike to the Santuari de Queralt, an 18th-century church which contains a much-venerated image of the Virgin. This sanctuary occupies a crag sometimes called the 'balcony of Catalunya', and offers far-reaching views across the mountains.

Pedraforca ('Forked Stone') is one of the most emblematic peaks in Catalunya. It presents a challenge for rock climbers, although there is also an easier hiking path to the summit. Picasso spent the summer of 1906 in **Gosol**, the little village at the base of Pedraforca, which is still a popular retreat for urbanites escaping the summer heat. Nearby **Saldes** is even closer to the hiking paths, and is another good base.

The Catalan Pyrenees

The picturesque Serra de Cadí range

Vall d'Aran

The Vall d'Aran (Val d'Aran in Aranese) is the only north-facing valley in the Catalan Pyrenees, a feature it shares with valleys on the French side of the mountain range. It is watered by the Garonne river, which empties into the Atlantic at Bordeaux, and its language, Aranese, is very similar to Gascon. For centuries it was almost entirely cut off from the rest of the world, but the construction of the Vielha tunnel in the 1940s linked it finally to the rest of Catalunya. And yet, it still feels remote and decidedly unlike anywhere else in the Pyrenees: Aranese, rather than Catalan, is the lingua franca, seen everywhere on street signs, and the traditional stone architecture has more in common with villages north of the border than the Mediterranean valleys to the south.

The interior of the church of Sant Climent

It's a very affluent little valley, boasting Spain's most glittering ski resort, Baqueira-Beret (a favourite with the Spanish royal family), and its capital, **Vielha**, is a smart little town full of upmarket boutiques and fancy restaurants. The single main road which runs along the base of the valley links a string of delightful villages containing some fine Romanesque churches. The valley is a wonderful walking destination, and its forests and mountains are home to an astonishing variety of wildlife, including myriad species of butterfly. (*See also pp140–41.*)

Vall de Boí

The beautiful, remote Boí Valley contains the greatest concentration of Romanesque art found anywhere in the world. Almost every village boasts at least one magnificent church flanked by a slender bell tower. Built between the 11th and 13th centuries, the churches stand testament to the wealth and prestige of the medieval counts who ruled the region.

There is an interpretation centre in **Erill la Vall** (*Centre del Romànic de la Vall de Boí, Camí del Batalló 5, Erill la Vall. Tel: 973 69 67 15*) which provides an overview of Romanesque art and architecture in the region. About a century ago, it was discovered that foreign buyers and museums were snapping up artworks from Catalunya's remote mountain churches. Fortunately, it wasn't too late to stop the exodus, and those that remained

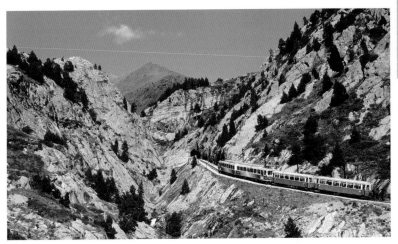

La Cremallera railway winds up through the Vall de Núria

were carefully transferred to Barcelona's Museu Nacional d'Art de Catalunya (National Art Museum of Catalunya), with reproductions of the frescoes being placed in the churches. The church of Sant Climent, in the village of Taüll, is the best known of the Boí Valley churches, thanks to its extraordinary depiction of the Christ Pantocrater (*see pp132–3*).

The beautiful and tranquil Boí Valley also offers a wealth of outdoor activities, from hiking in the stunning Parc Nacional d'Aigüestortes (*see p134*) to skiing in the resort of Boí-Taüll. You can also take the waters at **Caldes de Boí** (*www.caldesdeboi.com*), where the thermal waters are said to cure all kinds of ailments.

Vall de Núria

This lofty Pyrenean valley sits at around 2,000m (6,560ft) and can't be reached by private vehicle. Instead, visitors must take the delightful rack-and-pinion railway, called **La Cremallera**, which creaks up through magnificent mountain scenery. This valley has long been home to an important image of the Virgin (Núria is a very popular Catalan name for girls), now housed in the modern sanctuary complex of Santuari de Núria. The setting is breathtakingly beautiful; a verdant valley surrounded by huge, craggy peaks. It's a very popular ski resort in winter, and also offers all kinds of activities in summer, including horse riding, hiking, archery and mountain biking. There are restaurants and guestrooms available in the complex, and the website (*www.valldenuria.com*) offers some good-value packages which include a wide range of activities.

Drive: Vall d'Aran

This drive meanders through the eastern end of the hidden Vall d'Aran, allowing you to stop in traditional villages, admire Romanesque churches and enjoy some stunning views. It's best undertaken in late spring and early summer, as road conditions can be hairy in winter.

The drive covers about 31 km (19 miles) along the Vall d'Aran. There is no other route through, so you will have to drive back along the same road to return to the start.

Start in the Aranese capital, Vielha.

1 Vielha

This is a smart little mountain town which, despite the rash of new developments, has retained its charm thanks to strict building codes. The local architecture is stone, slate and wood, and has changed very little through the centuries. Stroll around the old town (signposted 'Eth Cap dera Vila') with its fine historic homes and the pretty little parish church of Sant Miquel.
Leave Vielha on the C28, heading east for 1.2km (³/4 mile).

2 Betren

This village on the outskirts of Vielha is huddled around its own Romanesque church (*glèisa* in Aranese), which has a very charming sculpture depicting a knight and his lady, and an elaborately carved portal. Betren has its own small ski station, Tuca Betrém.
Leave Betren on the C28, heading east for 1.4km (1 mile).

3 Escunhau

Escunhau is a steep, traditional village, with flower-filled balconies and another Romanesque church. This one has been substantially remodelled and boasts a very unusual portal, with geometric patterns. There is a fantastic signposted hike from the village, leading through forest to the beautiful Escunhau lake (about 9km/5¹/2 miles).
Continue in the same direction down the C28 for another 4km (2¹/2 miles).

4 Arties

This is one of the biggest and best known of the Aranese villages, and home to a very handsome *parador*. It's a chic little place, with slate-roofed houses overlooking the river, a couple of smart hotels, and restaurants.
There were once two castles in Arties: a single tower, high in the upper reaches of the village, is all that survives.
Continue in the same direction down the C28 for another 3km (1³/4 miles).

5 Salardú

Salardú once hosted a big market that vied with that of Vielha in the 13th century. Its former wealth is apparent in the size of the Romanesque church, still decorated with faint frescoes. It's another good walking base, with some fine hikes into the mountains.

Continue in the same direction down the C28 for another 1.2km (³/4 mile).

6 Tredòs

A mountain stream, crossed by an ancient bridge, rushes through Tredòs. Thanks to its proximity to the ski resort of Baqueira-Beret, the town is filled with holiday homes, but it's still tranquil outside the skiing season. A narrow road leads up to Banhs de Tredòs, where a little hotel (*www.banhsdetredos.com*) offers thermal water treatments.

Continue in the same direction down the C28 for another 7.5km (4¹/2 miles).

7 Baqueira-Beret

This modern ski resort provides the valley with much of its income, and is perhaps the most chichi resort in Spain. It's a favourite with celebrities and boasts luxury hotels and restaurants.

Continue in the same direction down the C28 for another 13km (8 miles).

8 Port de la Bonaigua

Until 1924, when this mountain pass was opened, the Aran Valley was entirely cut off during the winter.

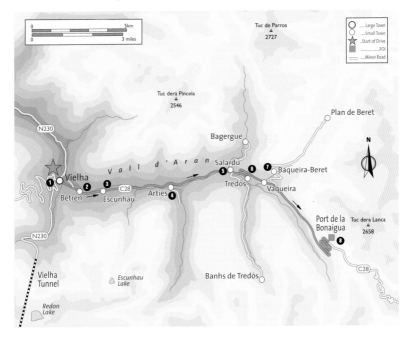

When to go

Northern Spain may be the greenest part of the country but it is also, not coincidentally, the wettest. Rainfall is heaviest in autumn and winter, but it's not uncommon in summer. Fortunately, this means that the magnificent beaches are comparatively uncrowded – except in August, when accommodation and flights are most expensive. Spring and early autumn are great seasons for walkers, and the Pyrenees offer a host of fantastic resorts for skiing and other winter sports.

Climate and weather

In general, Northern Spain is considerably cooler and wetter than the rest of the country, even during the summer months, but temperatures do not fluctuate as wildly as in the rest of Spain, so expect warm but not searingly hot summers, and mild winters in most non-mountainous areas. You should pack an umbrella and waterproofs throughout the year.

However, the size and geographical diversity of Northern Spain ensures considerable differences in climate depending on where you choose to visit. The mountainous regions, including the Pyrenees, the Picos de Europa and the Serra de Cadí, are considerably cooler than the coastline; snow covers the highest Pyrenean peaks well into May. Conversely, in the arid, desert-like

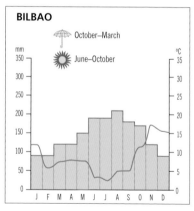

BILBAO

🌂 October–March

☀ June–October

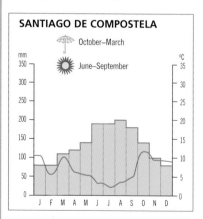

SANTIAGO DE COMPOSTELA

🌂 October–March

☀ June–September

WEATHER CONVERSION CHART

25.4mm = 1 inch

°F = 1.8 × °C + 32

landscape of the Bardenas Reales which encompasses much of southern Navarra, temperatures often top 40°C (104°F) during the summer months.

Seasonal sports and activities

Most Spanish winter resorts are concentrated in the Catalan Pyrenees and Andorra (*see 'Sport and leisure', p159*). They offer outstanding facilities for skiing (both downhill and cross-country), snowboarding and all kinds of other winter activities. The peak skiing season in the Pyrenees is usually from mid-December to early March, although ski resorts may be open from November to April.

Northern Spain is a fabulous destination for walkers, particularly in the Pyrenees and the Picos de Europa. The famous Camino Francés is the most popular of the network of pilgrimage routes which make up the Camino a Santiago. The best months to walk the Camino are May, June and September. July and August are extremely hot, particularly on the dusty *meseta* (plateau), and the pilgrim hostels fill up quickly because of the school holidays. However, July and August are good months to go walking in the Pyrenees and the Picos de Europa, but you should book accommodation in advance. Late spring and autumn are also great for walking, although your waterproofs will definitely come in handy.

July and August are, unsurprisingly, the best months for beach holidays, as there is least risk of rain. However, the most popular beaches can get extremely crowded (particularly in August), accommodation is harder to find, and prices are generally higher in most resorts.

Festivals, holidays and special events

Undoubtedly the biggest event on the calendar in Northern Spain is the Fiesta de San Fermín in Pamplona (early July), when tens of thousands of visitors pour into town to see the famous 'Running of the Bulls'. You will need to book accommodation several months in advance, and expect to pay a premium. Almost every town and village throughout the region has its own festival, many of which are concentrated in the summer months. We've listed the best of these (*see 'Festivals', pp20–21*), but tourist information offices and regional websites can provide comprehensive information.

You can only visit the Illas Cíes at Easter or in summer

Getting around

The easiest way to explore Northern Spain, especially if you want to get off the beaten track, is with your own transport. Although the region is well served by public transport, the network of buses and trains can be rather confusing for visitors, particularly those who don't speak Spanish. However, public transport is generally comfortable and inexpensive; it simply requires organisation. Tourist offices are almost always extremely helpful, and can provide information in several languages.

Independent travel by car

A car will give you the freedom to explore the most out-of-the-way places at your own pace.

With the drop in the cost of flights and car hire over recent years, it is probably cheaper to fly to the region and then rent a car. However, if you choose to bring your own car, you'll be pleased to know that Northern Spain is well connected to France and the rest of Europe by motorway, and the ferry ports of Santander and Bilbao provide regular links with the UK.

There are car rental companies at the airports, at some train stations and in all major towns and cities. All the large international firms are represented in Northern Spain, but you may find better deals with local firms. Shop around on the Internet and book well in advance if possible. Sometimes airlines offer discounts on car hire when purchased at the same time as the flight ticket.

Driving conditions and legal requirements

Road conditions are generally good. Motorists must drive on the right and the following speed restrictions apply: on toll motorways (*autopistas*) 120km/h; on non-toll motorways (*autovías*) 100km/h; on national roads 90 km/h; and in built-up areas and towns 50 km/h. The Guardia Civil (the Spanish police force which regulates traffic) can impose on-the-spot fines to drivers caught speeding.

It is compulsory for drivers to carry the vehicle registration document, a valid insurance certificate and a driving licence at all times. You are also required by law to carry a red warning triangle, spare headlight bulbs, a first-aid kit and a fluorescent safety vest. These will be supplied with hire cars, and can be purchased at most petrol stations.

Spain has some of the strictest drink-driving laws in Europe, with a limit of 0.5 milligrams of alcohol per millilitre of blood.

Fuel and toll costs

Petrol, while considerably more expensive than in North America, is less expensive in Spain than in most other EU countries. As elsewhere in Europe, petrol is more expensive at motorway service stations and usually cheapest at large supermarkets.

There are several toll motorways in Northern Spain. Prices are high, averaging between 3 and 8 cents per kilometre. However, the toll motorways are considerably emptier than non-toll roads and are very well maintained.

Public transport
By air

There are international airports at A Coruña, Asturias (Oviedo/Avilés), Bilbao, Girona-Costa Brava, Huesca-Pirineos, Pamplona, San Sebastián (Donostia), Santander, Santiago de Compostela, Vigo and Vitoria. The largest of these is Bilbao, which is the principal air gateway to the region. (Although Barcelona airport, a huge international airport on the Mediterranean coast, is not strictly speaking within the region covered by

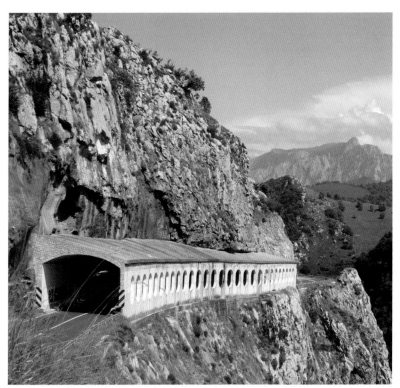

A road tunnel in the Picos de Europa

this guide, it may be convenient if you are beginning your exploration of Northern Spain from Catalunya.) The main airlines operating between these airports are **Iberia** (*Tel: 902 40 05 00. www.iberia.es*), **Air Nostrum** (*Iberia's regional airline. Tel: 902 40 05 00. www.airnostrum.es*), **Spanair** (*Tel: 902 13 14 15. www.spanair.com*), **Ryanair** (*Tel: 807 38 38 11. www. ryanair.com*) and **Vueling** (*Tel: 902 33 39 33. www.vueling.com*). Prices can be very reasonable if you shop around on the internet and book well in advance.

By bus

Northern Spain is covered by a comprehensive network of bus routes that link even the smallest hamlets with the main towns and cities. Bus services are particularly useful in the inland regions, which are rarely well served by trains. It's also worth noting that express buses are often quicker, cheaper and more comfortable than equivalent journeys by train. It's much faster, for example, to take the bus from Bilbao to Donostia-San Sebastián than the train. Regional bus services are provided by a host of different bus companies, which

The Santander train station in Bilbao

can be confusing at first. Fortunately, tourist information offices can usually provide up-to-date timetables that are invaluable for visitors. Most larger towns have at least one main bus station. Tickets for long-distance buses are usually purchased in advance at ticket booths within the bus station (each bus company has its own), but those for short routes can usually be bought from the driver on board.

All the larger towns and cities also operate municipal bus services. Bus timetables and routes are usually posted at bus stops but, again, tourist information offices can provide information on the most useful routes for visitors. Tickets can be purchased from the driver, although it's best to come prepared with small change. Single fares on city buses rarely top €1, and drivers may not accept bills over €10. City buses are increasingly well adapted for disabled travellers.

By metro and tram
Bilbao has an excellent metro system, designed by Norman Foster. It is clean, efficient, cheap, user-friendly and entirely accessible to wheelchair-bound travellers. Bilbao also has a modern tram system, inaugurated in 2002 and, like the metro, continually being expanded. Other Basque towns, including Vitoria-Gasteiz, are developing tram routes.

By train
The main Spanish railway operator, **RENFE** (*www.renfe.es*), runs most of the train services in Northern Spain. These services are supplemented in the Basque Country by **EuskalTren** (*www.euskotren.es*), which operates a slow but scenic service to Donostia-San Sebastián and beyond, and in Asturias and Cantabria by the **FEVE** line (*www.feve.es*), which runs along the coastline. Train services can be very useful in some areas and considerably less so in others. For example, there is a fast, regular RENFE train service along the Galician coast from Vigo to Santiago de Compostela, but there is no direct service from Santander to Bilbao (an express bus is considerably faster and more convenient).

Train tickets can be purchased in advance at ticket windows or from machines on platforms. Keep single journey tickets, as you may be entitled to a discount if you choose to make a return journey.

FEVE also runs a number of 'tourist trains', thematic tours that might include a visit to prehistoric caves, ancient mines, historic villages and more (*see www.trenesturisticosdelnorte.com*).

The **El Transcántabrico** is a very luxurious train, also operated by FEVE, which makes a week-long journey from León to Santiago de Compostela along the Bay of Biscay and recalls the golden age of opulent train travel in the early 1900s. The deluxe services include gourmet dinners, evening concerts, as well as excursions to the main sights along the route. Prices start at €2,600 per person (*www.eltranscantabrico.com*).

Accommodation

Northern Spain offers an excellent range of accommodation, with something to suit all tastes and pockets, from the glittering designer hotels of Bilbao to charming country inns in the Picos de Europa. Prices, unsurprisingly, reflect the facilities and location. Hotels in the popular seaside resorts are more expensive in July and August and may close down in winter. Some destinations, particularly Bilbao and Santiago de Compostela, are popular year-round, and you should book accommodation well in advance.

Hoteles, hostales, pensiones and fondas

Spanish hotels (*hoteles*) are awarded between one and five stars depending on the facilities available. Most will have lifts, en-suite bathrooms, and restaurants or dining rooms. *Hostales* and *pensiones*, which generally provide simpler and therefore cheaper accommodations, are rated with one, two or (very occasionally) three stars. However, the star-rating system doesn't take into account intangible factors such as service or charm, so you may find that a delightful *hostal* boasting all kinds of amenities except a lift and dining room rates a lower number of stars than an anonymous chain hotel in a city suburb. *Fondas* are traditional inns, which were once very basic, although the name has recently become fashionable for chic rural guesthouses.

Note that hotels may demand that guests spend at least a week, or choose the half-board option in summer (or in winter in the ski resorts) during the high season, so check in advance. Prices are usually cheaper at weekends and in August in the big cities (when there is no business trade), but more expensive during those periods in the seaside resorts or ski stations. Most of the hotels in ski resorts offer good packages throughout the year, which usually include bed and breakfast plus ski hire and lift pass in the winter, and bed and breakfast plus some kind of activity in the summer. These deals are often geared towards families and can be very good value. In general, it is almost always cheaper to book well in advance and shop around on the Internet. However, the current economic downturn has meant that there are also plenty of last-minute bargains to be had.

Although we have tried to list hotels with individual charm in the 'Directory', it may also be worth your while checking out the websites for the big Spanish chains. These can offer some surprisingly good bargains – particularly out of season, when you

A *parador* in Ordesa Natural Park

may find four-star hotels at the kind of prices you'd expect from a *pensión*. These big hotels may not ooze charm, but they are usually convenient, clean and boast excellent facilities.

Websites to check out include: *www.nh-hoteles.com*, *www.solmelia.com* and *www.abbahoteles.com*

Paradores

Northern Spain is very well endowed with *paradores*, the state-run hotel chain. *Paradores* often occupy extraordinary historic buildings, such as the magnificent 15th-century Hostal dos Reis Católicos in Santiago de Compostela. There are 11 *paradores* in Galicia; two in Asturias; four in Cantabria; one in Navarra; two in the Basque Country; and seven in Catalunya (although only four in the region covered by this book). The most emblematic *paradores* in Northern Spain (all in fabulous historic buildings or stunning natural areas) include those at Baiona, Pontevedra and Santiago de Compostela in Galicia; Cangas de Onís in Asturias; Santillana Gil Blas in Cantabria; Hondarribia in the Basque Country; Olite in Navarra; and Arties in Catalunya. Prices vary but usually cost around €70–100 per night, although the *parador* in Santiago de Compostela is usually at least twice that and must be booked many months in advance. There are a number of good deals available, including special discounts for seniors and youths.

Comprehensive information and an online booking service is available at *www.paradores.es*

Casas rurales and self-catering accommodation

Spanish *casas rurales* offer accommodation in rural areas and can be a wonderful way to experience Northern Spain. The range of accommodation offered is broad, from B&B in country farms to surprisingly luxurious rural hotels, self-catering cottages or rustic apartments. Some of the farms allow guests to participate in the harvest, get involved in cheese production or see the grapes being pressed for wine.

The regional tourist websites are a good source of information, while specific websites for finding *casas rurales* include *www.toprural.com*, *www.ecoturismorural.com* and *www.turismo-rural.com*

Self-catering accommodation is also very popular in seaside resorts. Many places offer flats or (occasionally) villas for summer

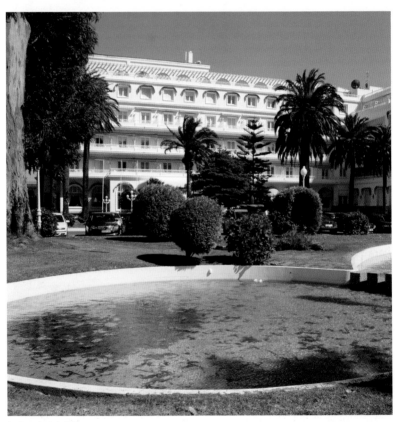

La Toca hotel, A Toxa

rentals. Local tourist information offices can provide information on reliable agencies.

Camping

Camping in Spain is permitted only at official campsites. The Spanish Tourist Office publishes an annual multilingual directory, the *Guía de Campings* (around €11), comprising a comprehensive list of campsites in Spain and their amenities. This information is also available at the official Spanish tourist website (*www.spain.info*).

Camping is very popular in Northern Spain, with numerous campsites throughout the region. These are graded according to a star system: four-star sites will usually have a pool, supermarket and restaurant, while establishments without any stars will be very basic but may be in very scenic locations. The website *www.camping-spain.net* is another useful resource.

Other accommodation (pilgrim hostels, mountain *refugios*, etc.)

Pilgrims walking the Camino a Santiago can stay at the very simple, cheap hostels or *albergues* provided for them along the route if they can show a *credencial*, sometimes called a 'pilgrim's passport'. This is issued by various pilgrims' associations in your home country and will be stamped at each hostel. The facilities in these hostels vary wildly: some will have kitchen facilities, others will have simple restaurants, and others will provide little more than a place to lay your head. Many of them also have curfews, or may expect pilgrims to depart early. Contact your local pilgrim association for information on the various accommodation options available for accredited pilgrims.

There are numerous mountain *refugios* scattered throughout Northern Spain. These range from extremely basic huts with bunk beds to modest inns with dormitory accommodation, showers and perhaps a simple café-bar or restaurant. The *refugios* are adminstered by the **Federación Española de Deportes de Montaña y Escalada**, and a comprehensive list, including descriptions, is available online at *www.fedme.es* (which has only a limited English section).

There are several official youth hostels in Northern Spain, and recently private hostels geared towards young backpackers have been opening up across the country. For information on youth hostels in the regions covered in this guide, see the website *www.hihostels.com*, which provides comprehensive information, including customer reviews, in English. To stay at an official youth hostel, you will need an international youth hostelling card, available from your home country or from the **Red Española de Albergues Juveniles** (Spanish Youth Hostelling Association, *Calle Castelló 24, 6º Derecha, 28004 Madrid. Tel: (+34) 915 22 70 07. www.reaj.com*).

Food and drink

Northern Spain is famous throughout the country for its outstanding cuisine. The Basque Country boasts the highest concentration of Michelin-starred restaurants in Spain, but you don't have to eat out at smart restaurants to appreciate the local food. Each of the eight autonomous communities described in this book has its own wonderful specialities, and discovering them is one of the greatest pleasures the region has to offer.

Regional specialities

In Galicia, tuck into the extraordinarily fresh shellfish plucked from the Rías, the delicious little green peppers from Padrón which have their own DO (*Denominación de Origen*), and finish up with the almond tart known as Tarta de Santiago. Asturias is also famous for its seafood, as well as rich bean-and-pork stews (*fabada asturiana*), which are washed down with local cider (*sidra*). Along with adjoining Cantabria, Asturias provides most of Spain's dairy produce, and you'll find a mouthwatering range of pungent cheeses (including the intense, blue *cabrales*). The Basque Country's top restaurants are among the finest in the world. The superb local produce is key to Basque cuisine, which emphasises fish and seafood dishes. The region is especially famous for the elaborate tapas that adorn every bar. The fertile fields of Navarra produce some of the best vegetables in Spain and superb artisanal cheeses are made in the mountains. A very popular local dish is river trout, cooked with potatoes and local ham. In the Pyrenees, succulent roast lamb and hearty stews are the main fare, and both regions also make excellent *embutidos* (cured meats).

Tapas

One of the great pleasures of Spain is to be found eating the tasty bar nibbles called tapas. Some of the dishes are particularly common in Northern Spain. In Galicia, *polbo á feira* (also known as *pulpo a la gallega*) is an extremely popular octopus dish, made with boiled octopus and potatoes and topped with olive oil and paprika. *Pintxos*, slices of baguette-style bread with different toppings, are very popular in the Basque Country. These may sound simple, but they can be extraordinarily elaborate. You might find, for example, *pintxos* topped with lobster and avocado mousse with a tomato confit, or wafer-thin slices of grilled aubergine topped with mushrooms and quail egg. The velvety anchovies (*anchoas*) plucked from the Bay of Biscay and deboned by hand are justly famous, although anchovies have become increasingly scarce in these heavily fished waters. Another local delicacy popular along the coast is the tiny eel (*angula*).

See also 'Asturian cider' (p55), 'Basque cuisine' (p76), 'Roncal cheese' (p94), 'The wines of La Rioja' (pp102–3).

Wine and cider

La Rioja is undoubtedly the most famous wine region in Spain. Although 85 per cent of the wines produced in La Rioja are red, there are also some excellent whites and rosés. Galicia's fresh white wines, particularly the Albariño wines of the Rías Baixas, are the perfect accompaniment to local seafood. Asturias and Cantabria don't produce wines, but Asturian cider is refreshing. The Basque Country is best known for its white wines, and its sharp, young *txacoli* wines complement local fish dishes. Navarra produces some excellent wines that, because they are relatively undiscovered, are usually less expensive. Catalunya produces some outstanding wines, including *cava*, the local version of champagne, and a wide range of reds, whites and rosés.

Where to eat

Restaurants (*restaurantes*) in Spain have a variety of different names. Inns may be called *mesónes* or *fondas* and are known for hearty local dishes, particularly *carnes a la brasa* (meat cooked over hot coals). *Marisquerías* specialise in shellfish, although most now also sell all kinds of seafood. Some tapas bars will also have a *comedor* (dining room) where more substantial meals are served. The traditional Spanish café-bar (known simply as a *bar*) is still going strong. Some *pastelerías* have cafés where you can enjoy coffee and cakes.

When and what to eat

The Spanish generally have a light breakfast, just a *café con leche* (an espresso with plenty of milk) and a pastry or a *tostada* (slice of toast) in the mornings. Lunch is the biggest meal of the day, and most Spanish restaurants offer a very reasonably priced set lunch (*menú del día*) on weekdays. Tapas bars fill up around 7pm, and dinner is generally eaten at around 9.30 or 10pm.

Markets

Fresh produce markets are still an intrinsic part of life in Northern Spain. In many coastal towns there is a fish auction right on the port. Covered markets generally open from 7 or 8am until around 2pm. Some reopen in the evenings from around 5pm to about 8 or 9pm. Note that fish stalls are almost always closed on Mondays. Most towns and villages, even the smallest, have a street market at least one day a week. Local tourist information offices can usually provide information on market days.

Entertainment

There's always something going on in Northern Spain, whether it's a lively village fiesta or a massive rock concert in Bilbao. Although other parts of Spain have a headier reputation for nightlife, the lively student towns of Northern Spain – especially Bilbao, Pamplona and Gijón – offer a good selection of bars and clubs. There's plenty of more traditional entertainment, too, from local festivals to football matches.

Opera, music and dance

All the big cities in Northern Spain (including Bilbao, Donostia-San Sebastián, Vitoria-Gasteiz, Pamplona, Santander, Oviedo, Gijón, A Coruña, Santiago de Compostela and Vigo) have theatres, opera houses or other grand venues which host a wide variety of drama (almost always in Spanish or in local languages), classical music, ballet and contemporary dance. The programme tends not to be restricted to classical music and dance, and even the largest venues also host live jazz, pop and rock concerts. Bilbao in particular attracts internationally famous companies from all areas of the performing arts, and the San Mamés football stadium is often used for major international rock concerts (including those of Madonna and Bruce Springsteen). There are also several excellent cultural festivals, including the Vitoria-Gasteiz Jazz Festival, the Donostia-San Sebastián Jazz Festival and the Santander International Festival (*see p21*).

Nightlife

Although Northern Spain is not as well known for its nightlife as other parts of Spain (such as Madrid, Barcelona or Valencia), the larger cities all have plenty of bars and clubs. A few of the summer resorts boast a lively nightlife during the high season, although the northern coast is better known as a quiet, family-friendly destination. Although bars and clubs tend to be concentrated in the larger conurbations, particularly those with a big student population, even smaller towns will have a few tapas bars with a lively atmosphere in the evenings. Live music is popular throughout the region, and even the smallest towns regularly host jazz evenings, or concerts dedicated to traditional music.

Local festivals

Every town and village in Spain celebrates at least one festival a year, the Fiesta Mayor, which is held in honour of the patron saint. For visitors, it's an ideal opportunity to join in with traditional dances or sports, try unusual local foods and watch processions and street concerts. Some of the biggest festivals in Northern Spain include the Tamborrada in San Sebastián (January), the Semana Grande (Aste Nagusia) in Bilbao (August), the Fiesta de Santiago Apóstol in Santiago de Compostela (July), and the Fiesta de San Fermín in Pamplona (July). (*For more information see 'Festivals', pp20–21.*) But don't overlook the smaller events in the region's most

rural villages, as these can be especially rewarding for visitors.

Bull-fighting

Bull-fighting has become increasingly controversial throughout Spain, and less than 30 per cent of Spaniards support it. In Catalunya the government is trying to ban the sport altogether. However, it still attracts a small following in some parts of Northern Spain, especially in Bilbao and Pamplona, both of which have historic bullrings.

Entertainment

A tapas bar in Bilbao

Shopping

Wines and local foods make fabulous gifts and souvenirs. You can pick up fine wines directly from producers, and have tasty nibbles vacuum-packed to take home. Numerous fashion labels started out here, including the Spanish chain Zara, now a worldwide phenomenon. Andorra is a mecca for duty-free shopping, but the most atmospheric way to shop is to head to local markets.

What to buy

Wines and local foods

Wines are easily available throughout the region, both directly from producers and from numerous fine wine shops. (Ask for recommendations – locals are generally very knowledgeable about their wines and love to talk about them.) Although the wines of La Rioja are the best known, you'll find excellent wines across Northern Spain. Remember that, with the recent restrictions on liquids in hand luggage, bottles of wine must be transported in your checked baggage. Shops are usually happy to wrap purchases in bubble wrap to ensure their safety, and many stores and wine producers offer an international delivery service for larger amounts. Most delicatessens can vacuum-pack (*envasado al vacío* in Spanish) cheeses and hams so that they are suitable for transporting in your suitcase. Other good foodie buys include Spanish olive oil and olives, which can be bought in tins for ease of transport. Although *paella* is not native to Northern Spain (it originates in Valencia on the Mediterranean coast), the rice dish has become Spain's national dish and *paella* pans or terracotta cooking pots (easily available from hardware shops, called *ferreterías*) can also make good gifts and souvenirs.

Spanish fashion

Spanish fashion is also a very popular buy in Northern Spain. The massively successful chain Zara (which sells modestly priced but highly fashionable clothes for men, women and children, and also offers a fabulous homeware range) was founded in Galicia. The upmarket designer Purificación García is also from Galicia, and the boutiques, which sell sleek, pared-down designs for fashionable women, can be found in every major town. The Hoss Intropia label is from the Basque Country, and offers beautiful, unusual fashion for women and children in gorgeous fabrics.

Souvenirs

In Galicia you'll find numerous souvenirs featuring the Celtic designs found on Galicia's ancient stone crosses and other monuments. A Basque favourite is the quirky label Kukuxumusu, which creates fun, amusing T-shirts and souvenirs, and has a special line of novelties depicting the San Fermín festival in Pamplona.

Duty free goods in Andorra

Andorra has become a big shopping destination, thanks to the absence of sales tax. Andorra la Vella, the national capital, contains scores of shopping centres and hypermarkets. These offer perfumes, beauty products, cigarettes, alcohol and all manner of other goods at bargain prices.

Where to shop

The big cities, unsurprisingly, have the widest range of shops, including all the popular Spanish fashion chains (Zara, Mango, Camper, etc.). But for delectable local goodies, such as cured sausages, honey and cheeses, you'll find local markets are the best bet (*see 'Food and drink', pp152–3*). If you want to pick up wines directly from the producers, local tourist information offices can provide information on *bodegas* that accept visitors or have shops open to the public. If you're in a hurry, the Spanish department store El Corté Inglés (with several branches in all the big cities) has a supermarket with a 'Gourmet Club' selling local delicacies.

You may want to stick to bottles as souvenirs!

Sport and leisure

Northern Spain is a paradise for anyone interested in outdoor sports and activities. Whether you simply want to laze on magnficent white-sand beaches or scale the challenging peaks of the Eastern Pyrenees, this region has something for everyone. It's particularly good for hikers, offering an incredible array of superb trails geared to walkers of all fitness levels.

Participatory sports and activities

Cycling

Mountain biking and touring is very popular throughout Northern Spain. Curiously, there are very few outlets that offer bike rental, so you may need to bring your own. It's worth asking at your accommodation if they have bikes available, as some hotels or *casas rurales* have bikes for guests. Some cities, including Bilbao, Donostia-San Sebastián and Logroño, offer a free or very cheap bike rental service to residents and non-residents alike.

Fishing

Special licences are required for both sea- and river-fishing throughout Spain, both of which are hugely popular in the north. Licences can be purchased from the **Federación Español de Pesca y Casting** (*www.fepyc.es*) or from **TeleLicencia** (*Tel: 902 30 06 22. www.telelicencia.com*).

Golf

Some of the best courses in Northern Spain include **Ulzama** (*www. golfulzama.com*) and **Castillo de Gorraiz** (*www.golfgorraiz.com*), both near Pamplona, **Fontanals** (*www. fontanalsgolf.com*) in the Catalan Pyrenees, and the **Real Golf Club de San Sebastián** (*www.golfsansebastian.com*).

Hiking

Northern Spain is a paradise for walkers, with superb hiking in the Catalan and Aragonese Pyrenees, the Picos de Europa and along the rugged coastline. A celebrated long-distance footpath, the GR11, crosses the Pyrenees from the Basque Country in the west to Catalunya in the east. Most famous of all is the network of routes comprising the historic pilgrim path, the Camino a Santiago. The most popular route on the Camino is the so-called Camino Francés (French Path), which enters Spain at Roncesvalles in Navarra and then loops down to

Pamplona, Burgos, León, Ponferrada and then on to Santiago.

Skiing and winter sports

Most Spanish winter resorts are concentrated in the Catalan Pyrenees, with ten ski stations equipped for downhill skiing and snowboarding and another seven specialising in cross-country skiing. You can find a full list of Catalan ski resorts at *www.catneu.net*. Andorra is another excellent destination for winter sports, with two enormous and well-equipped ski resorts (*www. skiandorra.ad*). There is also a small ski station at Alto Campoo in the Picos de Europa (*www.altocampoo.com*).

Watersports

All the main resorts along the northwestern coast of Spain have good facilities for a wide range of watersports. Most popular are sailing, windsurfing, surfing and kite-surfing, although the rough Atlantic seas make these waters best suited to experienced practitioners. Surfing is also very popular, and Northern Spain has often hosted the Spanish Surfing Championships (they were held in Gijón in 2008 and in Santander in 2009).

Spectator sports
Football

Football is the most important spectator sport in Spain (practically a religion!), and the region boasts several successful teams. Watching a match can be very exciting, especially in the Basque Country, where football is a peaceable focus for Basque regional identity. Athletic de Bilbao is one of the oldest teams in the country, with a huge following. In A Coruña, Deportivo de La Coruña is another strong Spanish team. Others include Osasuna de Pamplona, Racing de Santander, Sporting de Gijón, La Real Sociedad de San Sebastián and Celta de Vigo. Game tickets can be purchased easily (either directly from local stadia, or online from the websites of the bigger clubs), unless they're for major games, such as matches against Real Madrid or FC Barcelona.

Pelota

The Basque game of pelota (also called *jai alai*) is exciting to watch, as well as to play, and is played throughout the region.

Walkers in Ordesa

Children

The whole of Northern Spain is a massive playground. Kids can enjoy everything from a day at the beach, splashing and making sandcastles, to horse riding across the mountains or taking a thrilling ride down whitewater rapids in a raft. The region is a very popular destination for families and there is a wide range of accommodation, activities and sights geared towards family groups.

Child-friendly sights and museums

Most kids will find the ancient cave paintings at Altamira interesting (*see pp56–7*), and the museum has plenty of child-friendly interactive exhibits. The **Museo Jurásico de Asturias** dinosaur museum near Colunga in Asturias (*see pp54–5*) is another winner for younger kids. The **Domus**, in A Coruña, is a high-tech museum that will keep the family happy for a couple of hours (*Calle Santa Teresa 1. Tel: 981 18 98 40. www.casaciencias.org. Open: daily 11am–9pm. Admission charge*). Older teenagers interested in art will enjoy the contemporary art collections at **Artium** in Vitoria-Gasteiz (*see p79*), the stunning outdoor sculpture gardens at the **Chillida Leku Museum** (*see p77*) and, of course, the fabulous **Guggenheim Museum** in Bilbao (*see pp66–7*). There are fantastic **aquariums** in Gijón, Donostia-San Sebastián and A Coruña, which are always a good option to while away a rainy afternoon.

Outdoor activities

The beaches of Northern Spain are justly famous. You can play on long, golden sands and gentle waves, perfect for families with young kids, or discover secret coves by hiking along cliff paths if you are travelling with older children. Activities include everything from surfing to sailing. The Pyrenean ski resorts are extremely well equipped for children, who can take skiing and snowboarding lessons, try dog-sledding, or simply enjoy sledging in the special fun parks for infants and toddlers. These resorts also function in the summer, when activities might include archery and quad biking. Tourist information offices can provide comprehensive information. The Picos de Europa offer more fantastic opportunities for adventure sports, hiking and picnicking.

Where to stay

The most convenient and cost-effective way to explore the region with the family may be to rent a *casa rural*. As well as offering considerably more room than you'd get in a hotel, the cooking facilities can save time and money and are particularly handy for preparing baby food, picnics and quick breakfasts. Most *casas rurales* require a minimum stay of three nights. Larger hotels often have family rooms, and even smaller establishments may be able to offer connecting rooms.

Eating out

Visitors to Spain sometimes find it hard to adapt to the late dining hours, particularly if they are travelling with young families. Restaurants rarely open for lunch before 2pm, or for dinner before 9pm. Fortunately, tapas bars can fill the breach and they offer perfect,

child-sized portions. If you want a larger portion of something, ask for a *ración*. Even the fussiest children can usually find something they'd like to eat – *tortilla* (potato omelette) and *patatas bravas* (chunky fried potatoes) and platters of cheese or ham are perennial favourites. Most of the larger towns boast at least a couple of decent Italian restaurants serving pasta and/or pizza, as well as all the big international fast-food chains, if you cannot convert your kids to the local cuisine. Organic food is hard to come by, and organic baby convenience foods are virtually unknown, so bring supplies with you. However, you will find all the popular brands of formula baby milk in all pharmacies. High chairs are very rare, so bring a portable high chair if you need one.

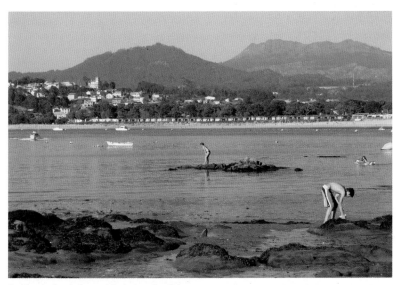

Hunting in the shallows at Praia America, Baiona

Essentials

Arriving and departing

By air

The main international airport in Northern Spain is Bilbao, which has direct flights with most European cities. Many visitors from outside Europe fly to Madrid and take a connecting flight to a regional airport (*for a full list, see 'Getting around', pp144–7*). The area covered by this book is extensive, and it may be most convenient to take internal flights between some destinations. The biggest Spanish airline is **Iberia** (*Tel: 902 40 05 00. www.iberia.es*), which operates most of the long-distance routes from Madrid, but numerous European carriers provide short-haul services between Northern Spain and other European destinations.

By sea

There are two international ferry ports in Northern Spain: Bilbao and Santander. **Brittany Ferries** (*www.brittanyferries.com*) operates services between Santander and Portsmouth or Plymouth in the UK. **P&O Ferries** (*www.poferries.com*) has services linking Bilbao with Portsmouth.

By rail

The main Spanish rail company is **RENFE** (*www.renfe.es*). It operates a number of international train services,

including direct sleeper trains between Madrid and Paris; Barcelona and Paris; Barcelona and Milan; and Barcelona and Zurich. There are onward connections from Madrid and Barcelona to major cities across Northern Spain.

Customs

There are no customs limits when travelling between EU countries, provided what you buy is for your own personal use. Visitors from outside the EU can bring in up to 1 litre of spirits, 4 litres of wine, 16 litres of beer and 200 cigarettes (or 100 mini-cigars, or 50 cigars, or 250 grams of rolling tobacco).

Electricity

The electricity supply in Spain is AC 220 Volts, 50 Hertz. Plugs have two round pins; power transformers and adaptors for different plugs are easily available in larger town and cities.

The scallop shell is the symbol of the Camino a Santiago

Internet

Internet connections are readily available in *cibers* (Internet cafés), cafés and most accommodation, particularly in the larger cities and seaside resorts. Wi-Fi is increasingly common across Northern Spain.

Money

Spain, like most other EU countries, uses the euro, which is divided into 100 cents (*céntimos* in Spanish). There are seven different bills: 5, 10, 20, 50, 100, 200 and 500 euros. There are eight different coins: 1, 2, 5, 10, 20 and 50 cents, and 1 and 2 euros. Local banks offer the best rates for changing money, although they charge hefty commisions. Cities have bureaux de change, which are open later, but offer less attractive rates. Credit and debit cards (which must be accompanied with photo ID) are widely used in larger shops, hotels and restaurants, but virtually never in museums or smaller establishments.

All ATM machines in Spain accept foreign bank cards, and most display instructions in various languages. Keep in mind that small, remote villages often don't have a bank, so cash-up in the larger towns. Withdrawing via a foreign credit card will incur a fee, which is not always denoted at the time of the transaction. Check your options before you leave home.

Opening hours

Most shops and businesses, including pharmacies, are open Monday–Saturday 9.30am–1.30pm and 4.30pm–8pm. Big department stores and chains don't close at lunchtimes and may stay open until 9 or 10pm. Most, but not all, museums close on Mondays and Sunday afternoons and only the biggest stay open at lunchtimes.

Passports and visas

EU citizens do not require visas to travel to Spain, although you will need a valid passport or photo ID card. Most non-EU visitors, including those from Australia, Canada, the USA and New Zealand, must present a valid passport and can remain in Spain for a maximum period of 90 days. All other visitors must apply to the nearest Spanish Consulate for a visa before travelling (*see www.spain.info*).

Pharmacies

Pharmacies are widely available and even the smallest villages boast at least one. They close on Sundays, and some may close on Saturday afternoons, particularly in summer, but all post a list of local *farmacias de guardia* (24-hour 'duty pharmacies').

Post

The Spanish Post Office, *Correos*, has several offices in every major town and city. Post boxes, like the post office logo, are yellow. Main offices are open Monday–Friday 8.30am–8.30pm, and 9.30am–2.30pm on Saturday mornings. Smaller branches don't open in the afternoons.

Public holidays

1 January – New Year's Day
6 January – Epiphany
March/April – Maundy Thursday and Good Friday
1 May – Labour Day
15 August – Assumption
12 October – Hispanic Day
7 December – Monday following Constitution Day (except in Castilla y León, Catalunya, Valencia, Madrid, Navarre and Basque Country)
8 December – Immaculate Conception
25 December – Christmas Day

Smoking

Smoking is still very common in Spain, and even those restaurants and bars which have non-smoking sections are generally smoky. Hotels, particularly the larger ones, may have non-smoking rooms or even non-smoking floors, but few smaller properties do. Public transport is, however, entirely non-smoking.

Suggesting reading and media

Good reads about Northern Spain include Mark Kurlansky's *The Basque History of the World*, a fascinating and quirky cultural history of Europe's oldest people. For a brilliant, concise overview of Spanish history, read *Spain: A History*, a collection of essays edited by Raymond Carr. *Everything but the Squeal: Adventures in Galicia* by John Barlow is a brilliant and hilarious introduction to the Galicians and their cuisine. And *Ghosts of Spain: Travels*

Through a Country's Hidden Past by Giles Tremlett is a perceptive and entertaining travelogue. There are several guides to the Camino a Santiago, but John Brierley's *A Pilgrim's Guide to the Camino de Santiago* is generally regarded as one of the most useful.

Tax

Sales tax is included in all purchases in Spain, but non-EU travellers can reclaim tax on purchases over €90. You will need to ask for a refund cheque when shopping, and then show it, along with receipts, to Customs at the airport when you depart (*see www.globalrefund.com*).

Telephones

Public payphones can be found throughout Northern Spain. Almost all are operated by Telefónica. Some function with coins, phonecards and credit cards, while others only accept phonecards (available in newsagents and tobacconists). Phone calls are pricey, particularly international calls. The cheapest way to call abroad is to purchase a pre-paid telephone card with a scratch-off pin number (these can be obtained in convenience stores and some Internet cafés).

All telephone numbers in Spain have nine digits which must be dialled in full, even if you are calling within the same city. To make an international call from Spain, dial 00, then the country code (1 for the USA and Canada, 44 for the UK, 353 for the Republic of Ireland, 61 for

Australia, and 64 for New Zealand), followed by the area code (minus the initial '0') and local number.

Most foreign mobiles can be used in Spain, although you should check with your network provider before travelling, and note that roaming costs can be very high. A Spanish SIM card can be bought in mobile phone shops in most larger towns and cities, but you will need to have a 'free' (i.e. unlocked) phone to be able to use it.

Time

The Spanish mainland is on CET (Central European Time), one hour ahead of Greenwich Mean Time (GMT).

Toilets

Public toilets (*aseos* or *servicios*) are few and far between. Good standbys include fast-food restaurants or department stores such as El Corte Inglés. Some bars won't mind if you ask to use their facilities, but it's becoming increasingly common for bars and restaurants to post up 'clients only' signs.

Travellers with disabilities

Facilities for travellers with disabilities are generally poor throughout Spain, but the newest museums (including the Guggenheim in Bilbao), hotels and restaurants are wheelchair-accessible, as is the Bilbao metro and most of the municipal bus network in the larger cities. Local tourist information offices can provide information on facilities for disabled visitors.

Essentials

CONVERSION TABLE

FROM	TO	MULTIPLY BY
Inches	Centimetres	2.54
Feet	Metres	0.3048
Yards	Metres	0.9144
Miles	Kilometres	1.6090
Acres	Hectares	0.4047
Gallons	Litres	4.5460
Ounces	Grams	28.35
Pounds	Grams	453.6
Pounds	Kilograms	0.4536
Tons	Tonnes	1.0160

To convert back, for example from centimetres to inches, divide by the number in the third column.

MEN'S SUITS

UK	36	38	40	42	44	46	48
Rest of Europe	46	48	50	52	54	56	58
USA	36	38	40	42	44	46	48

DRESS SIZES

UK	8	10	12	14	16	18
France	36	38	40	42	44	46
Italy	38	40	42	44	46	48
Rest of Europe	34	36	38	40	42	44
USA	6	8	10	12	14	16

MEN'S SHIRTS

UK	14	14.5	15	15.5	16	16.5	17
Rest of Europe	36	37	38	39/40	41	42	43
USA	14	14.5	15	15.5	16	16.5	17

MEN'S SHOES

UK	7	7.5	8.5	9.5	10.5	11
Rest of Europe	41	42	43	44	45	46
USA	8	8.5	9.5	10.5	11.5	12

WOMEN'S SHOES

UK	4.5	5	5.5	6	6.5	7
Rest of Europe	38	38	39	39	40	41
USA	6	6.5	7	7.5	8	8.5

Language

Spanish (Castillian) is the main language spoken throughout Northern Spain, but regional languages are also very important. Galego, Basque, Aranese and Catalan are widely spoken in their respective regions, and any efforts to speak even a few simple phrases in the local languages will be very much appreciated. English is not widely spoken, but here we've listed some common Castillian phrases to help you through most everyday situations.

PRONUNCIATION

Try to remember the following basic rules:

Consonants

c is soft before e and i (eg, Barcelona), but hard at any other time – **cómo**? (pardon?) pronounced 'ko-mo'.

g at the start of a word is a hard sound (as in get). In the middle of a word it is like the throaty 'ch' as in the Scottish 'loch' – **urgencia** (emergency) is pronounced 'err-hensi-ah'. In **agua** (water) it is hardly pronounced at all ('ah-gwa').

h is always silent – **hospital** is pronounced 'ospitahl'.

j is also pronounced like the 'ch' in 'loch' – **jamón** (ham) is pronounced 'ch-amon'.

ll is always like 'y' in 'yes' – **lleno** (full) is pronounced 'yay-no'.

ñ is like 'ni' in onion – **España** (Spain) is pronounced 'ay-spanya'.

qu is like 'k' in key – **Cuánto**? (how much?) is pronounced 'kwan-toe'.

r is rolled; **rr** is rolled even harder.

v is pronounced like a 'b'.

x is like 's' – **excelente** (excellent) is pronounced 'ess-say-len-tay'.

Vowels

a is a short 'ah' sound – **gracias** (thank you). It is never long as in the English 'gracious'. All the other vowels are long sounds. The letter **e** is a cross between the short English 'e' (as in get) and the long English **a** (as in grace) – **de** (of/from) is pronounced 'day' but in a clipped way. The letter **i** is a long 'ee' sound as in sí (yes), pronounced 'see', and **u** is like 'oo' in boot – **una** (one). The letter **o** is an 'oh' sound.

USEFUL WORDS AND PHRASES

yes/no	sí/no
hello	hola
good morning	buenos días
good afternoon	buenas tardes
goodnight	buenas noches
goodbye	adiós
please	por favor
thank you	gracias
you're welcome	de nada
today	hoy
tomorrow	mañana
yesterday	ayer
I am English	Soy inglés/inglesa
do you speak English?	¿hablas inglés? (informal) ¿habla Usted inglés? (formal)
very well/good	muy bien/vale
where is . . . ?	¿dónde está . . . ?
what/when	qué/cuándo
why/how	por qué/cómo
how much is . . . ?	¿cuánto vale/cuesta . . . ?
here/there	aquí/ahí
open/closed	abierto/cerrado
right	derecho/a
left	izquierdo/a
sorry!	¡lo siento!
excuse me (can I get past?)	perdóneme
excuse me (can you help?)	por favor
sir, madam, miss	señor, señora, señorita
I don't understand	no comprendo
I would like . . .	quiero/quisiera . . .
large	grande
small	pequeño
do you have . . . ?	¿tiene . . . ?
please write it down	por favor, escríbelo

DAYS OF THE WEEK

Monday	lunes
Tuesday	martes
Wednesday	miércoles
Thursday	jueves
Friday	viernes
Saturday	sábado
Sunday	domingo

NUMBERS

0	cero
1	uno/a
2	dos
3	tres
4	cuatro
5	cinco
6	seis
7	siete
8	ocho
9	nueve
10	diez
11	once
12	doce
13	trece
14	catorce
15	quince
16	dieciséis
17	diecisiete
18	dieciocho
19	diecinueve
20	veinte
21	veintiuno
30	treinta
40	cuarenta
50	cincuenta
60	sesenta
70	setenta
80	ochenta
90	noventa
100	cien
101	ciento uno/a
200	doscientos/as
500	quinientos/as
1,000	mil
2,000	dos mil
1,000,000	un millón

Emergencies

Emergency numbers

All emergencies: *112*
This is now the single emergency number throughout Europe, and is for all emergency services (fire, police and ambulance).

The Spanish emergency numbers are still in effect, but are redirected to *112:*
Ambulance: *061*
Fire brigade: *080*
Municipal police: *092*
National police: *091*

Medical services

EU citizens are entitled to free emergency health care thanks to reciprocal health agreements, but you will need to apply for a European Health Insurance Card in your home country before you arrive. Note that these agreements don't cover dental care and some other treatments, and private travel insurance is still recommended. Non-EU visitors should ensure that their own health care providers will cover them while abroad, or invest in private travel insurance before travelling to Spain.

For minor ailments, head to the nearest pharmacy. Spanish pharmacists are highly trained and can provide a number of over-the-counter treatments which are available only by prescription elsewhere. If you need to obtain prescription medication, bring a copy of your prescription as well as the generic name of the medicine you need.

If you require emergency health treatment, head to the nearest hospital (*hospital*) with an emergency department (*urgencias*). Hospitals are listed in the yellow pages (*Páginas Amarillas*).

Opticians (*ópticos*) are found in all larger towns and cities. They offer eye examinations, provide glasses and contact lenses, and can also do repairs.

Health risks

The main health risk in Northern Spain is excessive exposure to the sun, which can result in sunstroke. Ensure you use an effective sunblock, stay out of the sun at midday, and cover up if necessary. Be particularly careful with small children. Tap water is safe to drink, although bottled water is widely drunk.

Crime

Violent crime is rare in Northern Spain, but petty crime is common, particularly in the cities and in popular resorts. Pickpocketing and bag-snatching is the most common problem, so it's wise to be especially vigilant while on public transport, including on the airport buses. Leave valuables in your hotel safe if possible, and keep a copy of your passport and insurance documents separate from the documents themselves.

You can report robberies or accidents by telephone in English by calling 902 102 112. You will then need to sign papers in the local police station, but it will save long queues and avoid the strong possibility of being unable to find an English speaker who can help you.

Embassies and consulates

Australia

Embassy: *Plaza del Descubridor Diego de Ordás 3, 28003 Madrid.*
Tel: 913 53 66 00.
www.spain.embassy.gov.au

Canada

Embassy: *Calle Núñez de Balboa 35, 28001 Madrid. Tel: 914 23 32 50.*
www.canadainternational.gc.ca/ spain%2Despagne

Ireland

Embassy: *Ireland House, Paseo de la Castellana 46, 28046 Madrid.*

Tel: 914 36 40 93.
Consulate: *Calle Elcano 5, 48011 Bilbao.*
Tel: 944 23 04 14.
Consulate: *Edificio 'Los Sauces', Calle Alta del Puerto, 15401 Ferrol.*
Tel: 981 35 14 80.

New Zealand

Embassy: *Plaza de la Lealtad 2, 28014 Madrid. Tel: 915 23 02 26.*
www.nzembassy.com

United Kingdom

Embassy: *Calle Fernando El Santo 16, 28010 Madrid. Tel: 917 00 82 00.*
www.ukinspain.com
Consulate: *Calle Alameda Urquijo 2, 48008 Bilbao. Tel: 944 15 76 00.*

United States of America

Embassy: *Calle Serrano 75, 28006 Madrid. Tel: 915 87 23 03.*
www.embusa.es
Consulate: *Calle Juan Vieja 10, 15003 A Coruña. Tel: 981 21 32 33.*

Other cars are not the only danger in the Parque Natural Somiedo

Directory

Accommodation price guide

The accommodation price guide is based on the price of an average double room.

★	Less than €60
★★	€60–€100
★★★	€100–€150
★★★★	More than €150

Eating out price guide

The eating out price guide is based on an average-priced meal for one person, without drinks. As a general rule, restaurants are open for lunch from 1.30pm to 4pm and for dinner from 8.30pm to 11pm. They are often closed on Sunday evenings and Mondays.

★	Less than €25
★★	€25–€35
★★★	€35–€50
★★★★	More than €50

GALICIA

ACCOMMODATION

Costa Vella ★★
This delightful guesthouse is situated in a leafy garden just outside the remains of Santiago de Compostela's ancient walls. The 14 rooms mix traditional furniture with modern bathrooms and facilities (such as satellite TV) and there are a few period flourishes. Breakfast is served in the glass-enclosed terrace, which looks out over the ancient city.
Calle Porta da Pena 17, Santiago de Compostela. Tel: 981 56 95 30.
www.costavella.com

Xanela da Lúa ★★
Located in the traditional stone homestead in the Costa da Morte fishing hamlet of Lira (*see p38*), this small *casa rural* is incredibly charming, with simple rustic furniture and a pretty garden where (in warmer weather) breakfast is served. Your hostess Carmen can advise you on all sorts of activities in the area and has even been known to make her guests a traditional *queimada*, a potent combination of coffee and *orujo* (grape liqueur).
Calle Os Remedios, Lira. Tel: 981 76 13 06.
www.xaneladalua.biz

A Casa de Aldán ★★–★★★★
For those who like the cosiness of a *casa rural* but prefer something slightly more stylish, this new hostelry is a good choice. A leading architect has converted a former fish-preserving factory into a chic retreat overlooking the pretty Aldán bay in the Rías Baixas area. The décor is stylishly modern, with bold textiles and Scandinavian-style furniture.
Avenida José Graña 20, Aldán. Tel: 986 32 87 32.
www.acasadealdan.com

Parador de Santo Estevo ★★★
The old Benedictine

Monastery of Santo Estevo (or Ribas do Sil) has been converted into a luxury parador. Perched in the Sil Valley and surrounded by splendid, green countryside, much of the 18th-century architecture has been retained, while the rooms feature restrained modern elegance. There is a famed restaurant on site serving local specialities such as grilled trout from the Sil river and the local Ribera Sacra wines. As with all hotels in the parador network, check its website for great offers. *Nogueira de Ramuín, Ourense. Tel: 988 01 01 10. www.parador.es*

Hesperia Finisterre ★★★★
A Coruña's only five-star hotel is located next to the port and a five-minute walk from the old town. All 92 rooms, and many of the common areas, have a lovely sea view, and facilities are superb, including a state-of-the-art gym and spa, tennis court and free Wi-Fi access throughout the hotel.

Paseo del Parrote 2–4, A Coruña. Tel: 981 20 54 00. www. hesperia-finisterre.com

Parador dos Reis Católicos ★★★★
Santiago de Compostela's most celebrated hotel dates from 1499 when the 'Catholic Monarchs' commissioned it as a pilgrim's hospice. Located directly opposite the city's famous cathedral, its historic significance is unequalled and many cite it as the oldest hotel in the world. In comparison to its architectural opulence, the rooms, at least the cheaper ones, can seem a tad plain though comfortable enough, with antique furniture and all the facilities you would expect from a five-star hotel. *Plaza do Obradoiro 1, Santiago de Compostela. Tel: 981 58 22 00. www.parador.es*

EATING OUT
Mesón de Alberto ★★★
For traditional Galician fare, this is one of the most celebrated restaurants in the region,

manned by award-winning chef Alberto García and his family since 1975. Fish and shellfish are predictably its speciality. Try the sole with almonds, delectable hake *buñuelos* (a bit like a small fish fritter) caviar and salmon crêpe or whatever else is fresh in from the day's catch. *Rúa Cruz 4, Lugo. Tel: 982 22 83 10. www.mesondealberto.com*

Casa Marcelo ★★★★
Casa Marcelo is Santiago de Compostela's only Michelin-starred restaurant, run by esteemed chef Marcelo Tejedor. The cuisine is highly creative, evident in dishes such as an *amuse-bouche* of popcorn with foie gras, mussels in mango sauce, and crab with artichokes. The décor is warm and buzzing and, for an accoladed restaurant, prices are reasonable. *Rúa Hortas 1, Santiago de Compostela. Tel: 981 55 85 80. www. nove.biz/ga/casa-marcelo. Open: Tue & Wed lunch only, Thur–Sat lunch & dinner.*

Maruja Limón ★★★★

Another contemporary cuisine restaurant making waves in Galicia's rather traditional dining scene, Maruja Limón serves up playful, original combinations in an intimate setting. Try the tasting menu where you can expect dishes such as foie with apple ice cream, monkfish with confit artichokes, and mackerel in strawberry and cherry *escabeche* (cooked with vinegar).

Rúa Victoria 4, Vigo.
Tel: 986 47 34 06. www.
nove.biz/es/maruja-limon

Pablo Gallego ★★★★

This popular restaurant on the María Pinta square in A Coruña's old town is renowned for the freshest of seafood. Try the eels with eggs, St Peter's fish or *kokotxas* (grouper cheeks, a delicacy in many parts of Northern Spain) and choose from a cellar of more than 150 wines from all over the world.

Praza María Pinta 11,
A Coruña.
Tel: 981 20 88 88. www.
pablogallegorestauracion.
com

SPORT AND LEISURE

If you want golf, the club at La Toja in the Rías Baixas is one of the prettiest in the country, set on the edge of the mainland at O Grove and overlooking the Atlantic sea (*www.latojagolf.com*). Scuba diving can be learnt around A Coruña (*www.buceogalicia.com*) and horse-riding holidays can be booked following the Galician route of the Camino a Santiago (*www. caminoacaballo.com*).

ASTURIAS AND CANTABRIA

ACCOMMODATION

Casona de la Paca ★★

A handsome 19th-century mansion painted in vivid shades of ochre and umber, this is now a delightful rural hotel in the hills above Cudillero. It is set about 2.5km (1½ miles) from the beaches and is surrounded by extensive gardens filled with oak trees and magnolias. Choose between rustically decorated bedrooms for B&B accommodation, or self-catering apartments (popular with families) in a smart annexe.

El Pito, Cudillero.
Tel: 985 59 13 03.
www.casonadelapaca.com.
Closed: mid-Dec–mid-Feb.

Hotel Avenida Real ★★

Right in the historic centre of Villaviciosa, this little hotel offers nine cosy rooms and a wonderful suite. Staff are very welcoming, and the thoughtful extras – including delicious breakfasts with home-made pastries and the complimentary bottle of local *sidra* in every room – give this place a special charm.

Calle Carmen 10,
Villaviciosa.
Tel: 985 89 20 47.
www.hotelavenidareal.com

Hotel El Rexacu ★★

This tiny mountain inn, in a small hamlet in the Picos de Europa, offers plain but pristine rooms, rustically furnished with wooden beams and pale fabrics. The restaurant is excellent and serves unusual main dishes featuring locally reared ostrich.

Calle La Paloma, Bobia,

Cangas de Onís.
Tel: 985 84 43 03.

Hotel Gran Hotel Pelayo ★★★

This classic hotel overlooks the basilica at Covadonga, the most important shrine in Asturias. It's plush and luxurious, and makes an equally good base for a walking holiday in the Picos de Europa or a romantic getaway.
Carretera de Covadonga, Covadonga.
Tel: 985 84 60 61.

Hotel NH Palacio de Ferrera ★★★

A 17th-century palace, formerly the home of the Marqués de Ferrera, has been sumptuously converted into an elegant hotel. Although part of a chain, it feels more like a chic boutique hotel, with excellent service, a fine restaurant and a delightful garden. A bargain in low season.
Plaza de España 9, Avilés.
Tel: 985 12 90 80.
www.nh-hotels.com

Hotel De la Reconquista ★★★★

A favourite with visiting celebrities, this is possibly Oviedo's grandest hotel. A swish, contemporary building tucked behind the façade of a lavish 18th-century hospice, the hotel boasts every possible amenity, including a beauty centre and fine restaurant.
Calle Gil de Jaz 16, Oviedo.
Tel: 985 24 11 00. www. hoteldelareconquista.com

Hotel La Casa del Marqués ★★★★

This beautiful 14th-century mansion was built for the first Marquis of Santillana and is now a sumptuous boutique hotel. There are just 14 rooms, lavishly decorated with a mixture of antiques and modern furnishings, and the pretty gardens, tucked behind thick stone walls, offer countless secret corners to discover.
Calle Cantón 24, Santillana del Mar.
Tel: 942 81 88 88.

EATING OUT

La Marina ★

A popular, rustically decorated little tapas bar near Gijón's lively Plaza Mayor, with daily specials chalked up on the blackboard. Try the *chipirónes* (tiny fried squid), or the *patatas con cabrales* (potatoes with pungent Cabrales cheese), all washed down with the local *sidra* (cider) – poured, according to custom, from head height. It offers a well-priced set lunch menu from Monday to Friday.
Calle Trinidad 9, Gijón.
Tel: 985 34 62 46.
Open: Mon–Sat all day.

Oporto ★

For a truly mouth-watering range of *pinchos* (canapés), try this fabulous bar in the heart of Santander, near the cathedral. Get here before the crowds to admire the full range of wonderful toppings on display. The tomato confit with grilled goat's cheese is a winner, as is the wild mushroom *tortilla*.
Calle Lealtad 20, Santander.
Tel: 942 07 85 80.
Open: Mon–Sat all day.

Casa Camila ★★

A charming option in the hills overlooking Oviedo, this restaurant serves classic Asturian cuisine with a modern touch.

Try the traditional Asturian favourite, *fabada Asturiana*, a rich stew made with pork and white beans, or some freshly grilled seafood. Elegant rooms are also available.
Calle Fitoria 28, Oviedo. Tel: 985 11 48 22. www.casacamila.com. Open: Wed–Sun lunch & dinner, Mon lunch only.

El Bodegón ★★

An old-fashioned favourite in the heart of medieval Potes, this is a great place to fill up on hearty traditional home-cooking. It offers a great lunchtime fixed-price menu (Monday–Friday), which might feature dishes such as spring lamb or sturdy stews with spicy chorizo and beans.
Calle San Roque 4, Potes. Tel: 942 73 02 47. Open: Thur–Tue lunch & dinner. Closed: Wed.

El Molín de la Pedrera ★★

Both décor and cuisine display a fashionable mixture of cosy rusticity and contemporary style at this friendly family-run restaurant. Try its updated version of the classic Asturian bean-and-pork dish *fabada Asturiana*, or the delicious hake with clams, and finish up with one of the wonderful home-made desserts.
Calle Río Güeña 2, Cangas de Onís. Tel: 985 84 91 09. www.elmolin.com. Open: all day. Closed: Tue, Wed & Jan.

Gurea ★★★

This much-lauded restaurant is found in the pretty Cantabrian resort of Comillas and serves outstanding seafood as well as a few mountain dishes. Try the succulent fish baked in a crust of rock salt until the flesh melts in the mouth, or a local favourite, *fabes con almejas* (beans and clams), or perhaps even some game in season.
Calle Ignacio Fernández de Castro 11, Comillas. Tel: 942 72 24 46. www.restaurantegurea.com. Open: Mon–Sat lunch & dinner. Closed: Sun except in Aug.

Maruja ★★★

A long-standing classic in the fishing port of San Vicente de la Barquera, Maruja specialises in seafood dishes, particularly shellfish. The décor is sweetly old-fashioned, with flouncy curtains and polished wood, but the cuisine is decidedly sophisticated and is accompanied by a very good wine list.
Avenida Generalísimo 6, San Vicente de la Barquera. Tel: 942 71 00 77. www.restaurantemaruja.es. Open: Mon–Sat lunch & dinner, Sun lunch only. Closed: Wed in winter.

SPORT AND LEISURE

Cangas Aventura

Canyon descent, canoeing, whitewater rafting, horse riding, guided hikes, archery and more are offered by this adventure tourism company, based in Cangas de Onís, on the edge of the Picos de Europa.
Avenida Covadonga 17, Cangas de Onís. Tel: 985 84 92 61. www.galeon.com/cangasaventura

Escuela Cantabra de Surf

The beaches of Northern Spain are a mecca for

surfers. This long-established school in Somo (near Santander) offers lessons and summer courses. Classes are geared to students of all levels, from beginners to experts, and the school also offers equipment for rent.
Paseo Marítimo s/n, Somo.
Tel: 942 51 06 15. www.
escuelacantabradesurf.com
Real Golf de Pedreña
This 18-hole golf course, in a magnificent coastal location 25km (15 miles) from Santander, was co-designed by Seve Ballesteros.
Carretera General,
Marina de Cudeyo.
Tel: 942 50 00 01.

BASQUE COUNTRY

ACCOMMODATION

Hotel Ormazabal ★
A sweet, old-fashioned hotel in an 18th-century mansion in the heart of historic Bergara, this offers trimly kept rooms at a bargain price. The old beams, glassed-in gallery and original wooden staircase give it a traditional charm, while modern amenities include a café-bar.

Calle Barrenkale 11,
Bergara.
Tel: 943 76 36 50.
www.gratisweb.com/
hotelormazabal
Pensión Bellas Artes ★
The prettiest little *pensión* in town – so book well in advance. It's run by a charming mother-and-daughter team who go out of their way to make sure guests feel completely at home, with fresh flowers and complimentary chocolates. It is about a ten-minute walk from La Concha beach and the old quarter.
Calle Urbieta, Donostia-San Sebastián.
Tel: 943 47 49 05. www.
pension-bellasartes.com
Hotel Zubieta ★★
This traditional three-star hotel occupies some beautifully converted 18th-century stables set in gardens in the seaside resort of Lekeitio. It's handy for exploring the bewitching Matxitxako headland, and offers a choice of bedrooms or self-catering apartments that can sleep up to four people.

Lugar Portal de Atea,
Lekeitio.
Tel: 946 84 30 30.
www.hotelzubieta.com
Hotel Obispo ★★★
Tucked behind the old walls of Hondarribia, this hotel is located in the former bishop's residence. Each of the rooms are individually decorated with pretty prints and wooden furnishings, and some offer lovely views over the old rooftops. There's a small garden with a pretty terrace.
Plaza del Obispo 1,
Hondarribia.
Tel: 943 64 54 00.
www.hotelobispo.com
Palacio de Elorriaga ★★★
If you want the atmosphere of a country house with all the conveniences of a city on the doorstep, consider this charming hotel. It's set in a handsome 16th-century mansion about 1km (just over ½ mile) from the centre of Vitoria-Gasteiz, and amenities include a small gym and a wonderful restaurant serving local dishes.

Calle Elorriaga 15,
Vitoria-Gasteiz.
Tel: 945 26 36 16. www.
hotelpalacioelorriaga.com

Saiaz Getaria Hotela ★★★
A cluster of Gothic town houses has been converted into this enchanting little hotel, which is tucked away in the historic heart of Getaria. It's worth splashing out a little more for a room with wonderful sea views. The delightful staff can arrange all kinds of activities, including visits to the local *txacoli* wineries.
Roke Deuna 25–27,
Getaria.
Tel: 943 14 01 43.
www.saiazgetaria.com

Gran Hotel Domine Bilbao ★★★★
Right opposite the Guggenheim Museum, the Gran Hotel Domine is the city's slickest and most fashionable hotel. The interior was designed by Javier Mariscal, and the cocktail bar and restaurants are among the hottest addresses in town. There are stunning views of Gehry's beautiful 'titanium flower' from the roof terrace, where breakfast is served.
Alameda de Mazarredo 61, Bilbao.
Tel: 944 25 33 00. www.
granhoteldominebilbao.com

Hotel Londres y de Inglaterra ★★★★
This grand, belle-époque hotel has gazed out across the elegant curve of La Concha beach for more than a century. It remains one of the resort's grandest addresses, and boasts elegant rooms, the best of which have extraordinary views across the bay and out to the old town. Look for good deals on its website.
Calle Zubieta 2,
Donostia-San Sebastián.
Tel: 943 44 07 70.
www.hlondres.com

Eating out

A Fuego Negro ★
A modern bar, lined with bright contemporary art and popular with a hip young crowd, this serves outstanding, creative *pintxos*. Award-winning recipes include *txitxarro* (ewe's-milk cheese served with mint and cherry), but the menu changes constantly to reflect whatever produce is in season.
Calle 31 de Agosto 31.
Tel: 650 13 53 73.
www.afuegonegro.com.
Open: Mon–Sat all day.

Casa Urola ★
A long-established stalwart in the atmospheric Parte Vieja (old quarter), this friendly restaurant serves traditional Basque cuisine with some modern touches at surprisingly accessible prices. Downstairs at the buzzy bar you can tuck into a range of delicious tapas, or head upstairs to the tiny dining room for something more substantial.
Calle Fermín Cabeltón 20,
Donostia-San Sebastián.
Tel: 943 42 34 24. www.
restauranteurola.com.
Open: Mon–Tue &
Thur–Sat lunch and
dinner, Sun lunch only.
Closed: Wed.

Gure Toki ★
A classic Basque tapas bar, with platters piled high with all kinds of delicious tidbits, from traditional toppings to more elaborate pairings such as

wild mushroom with foie gras and prawns. You can also order more substantial *raciones* (large versions of tapas) – the *rabas* (a local word for *calamares*) are stupendous. It's also got a lively terrace overlooking the arcaded square.
Plaza Nueva 12, Bilbao. Tel: 944 15 80 37.
Open: Mon–Sat all day.

Baita Gaminiz ★★★

For a treat, book a table on the expansive terrace at this elegant restaurant. It enjoys views over the river, and is found conveniently close to Bilbao's Guggenheim Museum. Outstanding contemporary Basque cuisine is on offer with a constantly changing menu featuring the freshest seasonal produce. It also boasts a fabulous gourmet shop, where you can pick up delicacies to take home.
Calle Mazarredo Zumardia 20, Bilbao. Tel: 944 24 22 67. Open: Mon lunch only, Tue–Sat lunch and dinner.

Cube ★★★

The most daring building in Vitoria-Gasteiz, the museum of contemporary art (called the Artium), contains a sleek designer restaurant. It serves light snacks and breakfasts, or you can dine more substantially on sophisticated fusion cuisine such as cod with cardamom yogurt, asparagus and shitake mushrooms, or roast suckling pig with apple and hazelnut praline.
Museo Artium, Calle Francia 24, Vitoria-Gasteiz.
Tel: 945 20 37 28.
www.cubeartium.com

Kaia ★★★

For the freshest of fish and wonderful views over Getaria's working port, this restaurant can't be beaten. Choose from the more formal dining rooms upstairs or the casual brasserie downstairs, where you can watch your fish being prepared barbecue-style on hot coals. Book one of the pretty tables out on the terrace – particularly romantic when candle-lit in the evenings.
Calle General Arnau 4, Getaria. Tel: 943 14 05 00. www.kaia-kaipe.com

Open: daily for lunch & dinner.

Sebastián ★★★

This restaurant occupies premises which once belonged to an old-fashioned grocery store, and it has kept the original façade. Inside, it's prettily decorated with prints, flowers and burnished mirrors. Traditional Basque cuisine is on the menu, including *marmitako* (fish stew), and you can finish up with scrumptious home-made desserts.
Calle Mayor 11, Hondarribia.
Tel: 943 64 01 67. www. sebastianhondarribia.com.
Open: Tue–Sat lunch & dinner, Sun lunch only.

Zallo Barri ★★★

An elegant lunch spot in Gernika, and a short walk from the centre of the old town, this restaurant serves refined Basque cuisine prepared with carefully sourced local ingredients. It offers a series of good-value set menus as well as upmarket tapas and *raciones*.
Calle Juan Calzada 79, Gernika.

Tel: 946 25 18 00.
www.zallobarri.com.
Open: daily for lunch &
dinner.

Mugaritz ★★★★
Chef Andoni Aduriz
apprenticed with Ferran
Adrià at El Bulli, and his
cuisine is every bit as
exciting and inventive as
you might expect. There
are two tasting menus
available, which
showcase extraordinary
dishes such as hake fillet
with baby garlic,
hazelnut praline, soured
cream and bitter flowers.
The restaurant is located
in a rustic stone
farmhouse surrounded
by gardens about a 30-
minute drive from
Donostia-San Sebastián,
and was voted in 2009
the fourth-best
restaurant in the world
by *Restaurant* magazine.
Aldura aldea 20,
Errenteria.
Tel: 943 52 24 55.
www.mugaritz.com

Entertainment
Bilborock
A 17th-century Baroque
church makes an unusual
setting for this popular
live-music venue, run by

Bilbao city council. As
well as a regular
programme of music,
theatre and film events, it
hosts an annual pop rock
music competition, open
to new bands from across
Europe.
Muelle de la Merced 1,
Bilbao.
Tel: 944 15 13 06.
www.bilbao.net/bilborock

Teatro Arriaga
Bilbao's prestigious
theatre and opera house
hosts an excellent
programme of classical
music, ballet and opera.
Plaza de Arriaga, Bilbao.
Tel: 944 79 20 36.
www.teatroarriaga.com

NAVARRA
Accommodation
Albergue Nuestra
Señora del Yugo ★
Located in an old
hermitage on the edge of
the Bardenas Reales in
the village of Arguadas,
this hostel is popular
with hikers and cyclists
and has bunk beds and
shared bathrooms. Full
board available.
Plaza San Esteban 6,
Arguadas.
Tel: 948 38 60 11.
www.virgendelyugo.com

Camping Osate ★
On the northern
outskirts of Ochagavia
(but a mere five-minute
walk from the village),
this superior campsite is
as clean as a whistle and
is laid out over grassy
lawn with ample trees to
provide shade. Also on-
site are a number of
natural wood cabins, all
equipped with linen and
cooking facilities, heating
and small porches to
hang out on and enjoy
the mountain air.
Carretera NA130
(signposted from the
village), Ochagavia.
Tel: 948 89 01 84.
www.campingosate.net

Casa de Beneficiados ★
This pilgrim's hospice
dates from the 18th
century and is adjacent
to the Colegiata Real in
Roncesvalles. A recent
facelift has seen it
stripped back and
simplified, featuring
lots of natural wood
beams and floors,
exposed brick walls and
natural textiles and
furniture that are more
Scandinavia than Spain.
All rooms have their own
kitchen and bathroom.

Colegiata Real,
Roncesvalles.
Tel: 948 76 01 05. www.
casadebeneficiados.com

Sueldegia ★

This well-established guesthouse near the main square in the village – a stone's throw from Zugarramurdi's famous 'witches' caves' – will never win any design awards, but its host Iñaki will make you feel incredibly welcome and is an authority on local folklore. The spacious rooms are comfortable enough, with mix-and-match furniture and private bathrooms. A pretty patio-garden brightens things up considerably.

Calle Lapizteguia,
Zugarramurdi.
Tel: 974 59 90 88.

Txarpa Etxea ★

Many homesteads in the Roncal Valley have been converted to *casas rurales*, but this one, located opposite the river in the village of Roncal, stands out for its welcoming hostess and pretty attic rooms with exposed beams and bright, homespun décor.

There is a cosy common area for chilling out or watching TV, and breakfast is provided in the bar downstairs. Bathrooms are shared, but at these prices, who's complaining?

Calle Mayor, Roncal.
Tel: 948 47 50 68.

Hotel Castillo de Javier ★★

The Calle San Nicolás in Pamplona is the main drag for great tapas bars and not-so-great hostels. This new hotel has a slightly generic feel and small-ish rooms, but the facilities are good and it's certainly a step up from its neighbours. A good choice if you want to spend a bit more money for a night away from the backpacker scene.

Calle San Nicolás 50–52,
Pamplona.
Tel: 948 20 30 40. www.
hotelcastillodejavier.com

Hotel Xabíer ★★

Located in the same peaceful grounds as the Castillo de Javier (*see above*), this lovely hotel is full of period touches: antiques, throws and rugs adorn the rooms

and a charming restaurant with a terrace is on the ground floor – a fine spot from which to admire the castle's impressive battlements and towers.

Castillo de Javier, Javier.
Tel: 948 88 40 06.
www.hotelxabier.com

Aires de Bardenas ★★★★

For one of Spain's most exciting new destination hotels, Barcelona-based architects Emiliano López and Mónica Rivera have created a cluster of minimalist, metal-clad cabins that rest beautifully within the incredible desert landscape of the Bardenas Reales. Most have a private patio, adorned with a fruit tree, and some have outside circular baths. Each cabin has an enormous pop-out window deep enough to accommodate a built-in day-bed and wide enough to beautifully frame the desert horizon. Strong winds are constant in the Bardenas Reales, and to protect their work (and guests) the architects have placed a windbreak made of wooden crates around the hotel, an ingenious invention that borders on land art. The hotel has its own vegetable garden and its produce, including the famous *cogollos* (lettuce hearts) from the region, is used in the in-house restaurant.

Carretera de Ejea, Km 1.5, Tudela. Tel: 948 11 66 66. www.airedebardenas.com

EATING OUT

Bar Gaucho ★

Though not of the same standard as in San Sebastián, Pamplona's reputation for creative tapas and *pintxos* (Basque tapas) is growing. Bar Gaucho is a good exponent, with mouthwatering morsels such as stuffed anchovies, solomilo with Roquefort sauce, sea urchins, duck terrine and 'scrambled' black sausage.

Calle Espoz y Mina, Pamplona. Tel: 948 22 50 73. www.cafebargaucho.com

Altzatenea ★★

There is only a handful of bars and restaurants in Zugarramurdi. This is one of the best, offering succulent grilled lamb chops and steaks and a good selection of local wine. The interior décor is slightly antiquated (not in a good way), but on warmer nights you can choose to dine on their pretty, flower-filled terrace.

Calle Basaburua 3, Zugarramurdi. Tel: 974 59 90 88.

Restaurante 33 ★★★

The town of Tudela is famous for its vegetables and this prize-winning restaurant serves nothing but the freshest and finest. Although it's not strictly a vegetarian eatery, as much attention is given to vegetables as to meat – a rare thing in these parts. Try the artichoke hearts filled with foie, monkfish with *pochas* (giant white beans), or roast potatoes stuffed with potato 'cream' and Iberian ham.

Calle de los Capuchinos 7, Tudela. Tel: 948 82 76 06. www.restaurante33.com

Rodero ★★★★

The elegant Rodero is considered one of Pamplona's finest restaurants, presenting sophisticated cuisine using local ingredients. Dishes using asparagus – Navarra's star vegetable – are always on the menu. Other surprises include cheese and peanut 'nougat' with foie, a 'jelly' of *percebes* (goose barnacles) and deconstructed 'sweet' *paella*. The tasting menu is very reasonable and a good way to sample what's on offer.

Calle Emilio Arrieta 3, Pamplona. Tel: 948 22 80 35. www. restaurantorodero.com

SPORT AND LEISURE

The Vías Verdes ('Green Ways') is a network of popular walking and cycling routes over disused railway tracks. There are four in Navarra, including a trek around the incredible Foz de Lumbier (Lumbier Gorge) near Sangüesa, and the Bera Valley near Zugarramurdi. Check out *www.viasverdes.com* or ask at any tourist information office for a map.

LA RIOJA

Accommodation

Don Cosme Palacio ★★
The old 18th-century *bodega* of respected winemakers has been converted into a small yet charming guesthouse with rustic chic décor and views of the surrounding vineyards. Breakfast and evening meals are served in a pretty, plant-filled winter garden.
Carretera de Elciego, Laguardia.
Tel: 945 60 02 10.

La Posada de San Millán ★★
This stylish *casa rural* occupies the same grounds as the famous Yuso monastery. Rooms are spacious and stylish, with wrought-iron beds, stripped wood furnishings and antique fittings. Although it's located very near the main car park, the area becomes beautifully quiet after the monastery closes, allowing you to enjoy the amazing countryside.
Calle Prestiño 5, San Millán de la Cogolla.
Tel: 941 37 31 61.
www.ascarioja.es/laposada

Senorío de Casalarreina ★★
Part of the excellent Rusticae group that specialises in stylishly renovated country retreats, this lovely guesthouse, located about 8km (5 miles) from Haro on the road to Ezcaray, is adjacent to the Nuestra Señora de la Piedad monastery. Rooms feature exposed beams, stone walls and quaint wall murals, and some have Jacuzzis.
Plaza Santo Domingo de Guzmán 6, Casalarreina.
Tel: 941 32 47 30.
www.rusticae.es

Hotel-Baleanario Arnedillo ★★★
Recently renovated, this spa hotel is nestled in the sierra of La Rioja Baja, near the River Cidacos. All manner of water-based treatments are on offer, from thermal baths, to different types of whirlpools and water jets, to mud wraps and massages. A pool overlooks the valley and rooms have been tastefully modernised; some have terraces with splendid vistas.
Calle Joaquín Velasco, Arnedillo.
Tel: 941 39 40 00.

Hotel Echaurren ★★★
Despite its rather stately, medieval appearance, this family-run hotel is warm and welcoming and, during winter, the epicentre of Ezcaray's buzzing ski scene. Rooms are classically comfortable (without being stuffy) and there are two excellent restaurants on site (*see listing below*). Downstairs is a lounge with an open fireplace, a fine place to curl up with a book when the wind whips through the Sierra de la Demanda.
Calle Padre José García 19, Ezcaray.
Tel: 941 35 40 47.
www.echaurren.com

Hotel Villa de Laguardia ★★★
Don't be deceived by its modern appearance: this hotel specialises in old-fashioned hospitality. Rooms are spacious (some have views of the Sierra de Cantabria) with contemporary, tasteful décor, and the in-house restaurant is superb. A spa

specialising in *vinoterápia* (treatments using wine-based products) is a new addition.

Paseo de San Raimundo 15, Laguardia.
Tel: 945 60 05 60. www. hotelvilladelaguardia.com

Hotel Marqués de Riscal ★★★★

Frank Gehry's titanium-clad destination hotel, located in the grounds of the Marqués de Riscal *bodega* in the tiny village of Elciego, is nothing short of extraordinary and is an experience that, budget permitting, should not be missed. The in-house spa – run by the French Caudalie group – is a pioneer in vinotherapy treatments (using grape-based products) and the restaurant is superb (*see listing below*). Rooms are more spacious in the annexe, which looks out over the vineyards. In the main structure the rooms feature more of Gehry's quirky geometry, with curved walls and off-kilter, steeple-shaped ceilings, and some have views of the impressive village church. The hotel is off-limits to the general public, and allows entry only to guests or those booked into the spa or restaurant.

Calle Torrea 1, Elciego.
Tel: 945 18 08 88.
www.marquesderiscal.com

EATING OUT

La Canada ★

This buzzing little roadside shack is located on the main road just before you reach the village of Anguiano in the Sierra de la Demanda, and serves up hearty bacon-and-egg breakfasts and cooked lunches. There are a few tables in the outdoor garden, right next to the chicken coop!

Carretera Anguiano, Km 49.
Tel: 941 74 50 03.

El Mirador ★★

Refuel after visiting the Yuso and Suso monasteries at this no-nonsense restaurant, a few kilometres from San Millán de la Cogolla in the village of Berceo. Walk through the bar area to the dining room, which has a large look-out window over the surrounding countryside and Nájera river, and order local favourites such as *patatas a la riojana or pimientos rellenos* (red peppers stuffed with meat or fish).

Carretera de San Millán, Berceo.
Tel: 941 37 30 08.

El Portal and El Echaurren ★★★★

Both these restaurants are located inside the excellent family-run Hotel Echaurren (*see listing above*) and each have a very different personality. El Echaurren, run by Marisa Paniego, specialises in exquisitely prepared local specialties in a traditional setting, and is said to serve the finest croquettes in Northern Spain (they can be tried as part of the *menu del día*, which is particularly good value). Marisa's son Francis is at the helm of El Portal, a creative take on local cuisine with surprising flavours and combinations.

Calle Padre José García 19, Ezcaray.

Tel: 941 35 40 47.
www.echaurren.com

Restaurante Marqués de Riscal ★★★★

Part of Frank Gehry's extraordinary titanium complex for the Marqués de Riscal winery, this outstanding restaurant features superb contemporary cuisine by award-winning chefs Francis Paniego (also head chef at El Portal in Ezcaray, see listing above) and José Ramón Piñeiro. Traditional dishes such as roast suckling pig have been updated, and are paired with an outstanding wine list.

Calle Torea 1, Elciego.
Tel: 945 18 08 80.
www.marquesderiscal.com

SPORT AND LEISURE

The Vinobús

From July–November a jaunty little bus takes you through the vineyards of La Rioja and some of the region's principal stop-offs on the Camino a Santiago. The bus leaves from Logroño's tourist information office.

Tourist office, Paseo del Espolón 1, Logroño.

Tel: 902 27 72 00.
www.lariojaturismo.com/vinobus

THE ARAGONESE PYRENEES

ACCOMMODATION

Camping Municipal Peña Sola ★

Located in the village of Agüero, this neat little campsite lies at the base of the Peña Sola, a massive rocky overhang that is part of the Mallos de Riglos chain (see p120). Services are basic, though there is a lively bar (it's a favourite with locals) and a good swimming pool.

Carretera 534, Agüero.
Tel: 974 38 05 33.

Posada Magoria ★

Located in the beautiful village of Ansó, this guesthouse has been lovingly restored by a local couple. Rustic charm abounds, with stripped-back wooden and stone walls, exposed beams, antique furniture and crisp white sheets. At the rear, a pretty garden overlooks the valley, and in the evenings, vegetarian meals are served using organic, local produce.

Calle Milagro 8, Ansó.
Tel: 974 37 00 49.
www.posadamagoria.com

Hospedería de Loarre ★★

Hospederías are local government-run inns located in historic buildings (a bit like a less grand version of a parador). In Loarre, the hospedería is located in the main square and has 12 cheerful rooms and a fine restaurant on the ground floor. Good-value meal and accommodation packages are available and picnics can be prepared with advanced notice.

Plaza Miguel Moya 7, Loarre.
Tel: 974 38 27 06. www.hospederiasdearagon.com

Hotel Barosse ★★

Located in a residential area a few kilometres from the centre of Jaca, this lovely guesthouse, which feels more like a private home, is run by two charming hosts who go out of their way to make you feel welcome. Rooms have been decorated eclectically, with pretty, oriental-inspired objects and furnishings, and there is a sauna and Jacuzzi on the lower floor. Massages from a local therapist can also be arranged.

Calle Estiras 4, Barós, Jaca. Tel: 974 36 05 82. www.barosse.com

Hospedería San Juan de la Peña ★★★

Part of the 17th-century (or 'new') monastery of San Juan de la Peña (*see pp118–19*) has been converted into a modern hotel. A daring sheet of curtain glass has replaced old stonework on an outer wall, allowing natural light into most of the 20 rooms (four are duplexes), which have been decked out in tasteful contemporary décor with a few bold touches. But the surroundings are the real winner, especially the mountain views from the woods behind the monastery.

Monasterio de San Juan de la Peña. Tel: 974 37 44 22. www. hospederiasdearagon.com

EATING OUT

Casa d'Caminero ★

The village of Loarre, which lies at the gateway to the incredible Castillo de Loarre (*see p116*) has just a handful of restaurants and, going by the crowds lining up for tables, this must be one of the best. Home-cooking using local ingredients is the attraction, with succulent baby lamb chops, roast game and monster salads from the *huerta* (vegetable garden).

Plaza San Pedro 14, Loarre. Tel: 974 36 07 42.

Casa Fau ★

Located directly opposite the entrance to Jaca's cathedral, this traditional tapas bar is a Jaca institution. Tapas, such as wild mushrooms, delicious *pinchos* (canapés) and *pimientos del Padrón* (Padrón peppers) are piled high on platters at the bar, or seafood can be grilled to order. There is an outdoor terrace on a lovely square.

Plaza Catedral 6, Jaca. Tel: 974 36 15 94.

Restaurante Gaby ★★★

This restaurant is considered the finest in the Hecho Valley.

Located in a pretty homestead in the village of the same name, Gaby is a renowned chef and a specialist in regional cooking. Her restaurant is highly personal, more like eating in her own dining room, with mountain memorabilia and lacework made by Gaby herself. Upstairs is a handful of rooms with the same homespun décor, should you wish to stay the night. Booking ahead is advised.

Plaza Palacio 1, Hecho. Tel: 974 37 50 07. www.casablasquico.com

SPORT AND LEISURE

UR Pirineos

Mountain sports are big in this part of the Pyrenees, and UR Pirineos offers rafting, canoeing, kayaking and canyoning. It has two offices:

Avenida 1ª Viernes de Mayo 14, Jaca. Tel: 974 35 67 88.
Carretera A132, Km 38, Murillo de Gallego. Tel: 974 38 30 48. www.urpirineos.es

THE CATALAN PYRENEES

ACCOMMODATION

Hostal Rural Santa Maria ★★

A traditional mountain inn built of stone and wood in a breathtaking rural village, this is run by a very welcoming family. It's a perfect base for skiing in winter, for hiking in the spectacular National Park of Aigüestortes, or for exploring the rich Romanesque heritage of the Boí Valley. Smoking is not permitted in the rooms.

Plaça Cap del Riu 3, Taüll.
Tel: 973 69 61 70.
www.taull.com

Hotel El Ciervo ★★

Tucked away in the old quarter of the Aranese capital of Vielha, this little inn boasts a brightly painted façade and traditional wooden balconies. Family-run and cosy, it offers prettily decorated rooms and delicious, plentiful breakfasts.

Plaça Sant Orenç 3, Vielha.
Tel: 973 64 01 65.
www.hotelelciervo.net

Hotel Roca Blanca ★★

An elegant, modern hotel which has been built of local materials to blend in with the rural surroundings, this offers a range of activities, including whitewater rafting, canoeing, winter sports and guided tours of the region. It's located in Espot, one of the gateways to the National Park of Aigüestortes, and is close to a ski resort.

Carrer Església, Espot.
Tel: 973 62 41 56.
www.rocablanca.net

Hotel de Tredòs ★★

This chalet-style hotel is close to the slopes of Baqueira-Beret, but it's also a popular summer retreat thanks to its gardens and outdoor pool. It has good-value family rooms, and serves tasty local mountain dishes in the restaurant.

Carretera Vielha-Baqueira, Km 177.5, Tredòs.
Tel: 973 64 40 14.
www.hoteldetredos.com

El Sport Wellness Mountain Spa ★★

This large, well-equipped, chalet-style hotel sits right at the base of the slopes in Soldeu. It offers spacious rooms, a spa, sauna, restaurant and all manner of facilities for outdoor activities throughout the year.

Soldeu, Andorra.
Tel: 376 87 06 00.
www.sportwellness.ad

Hotel Casa Estampa ★★★

This charming, traditional inn in the pretty Aranese village of Escunhau has been recently overhauled to upgrade its status from hostel to hotel. Considerably more luxurious now (amenities include a small indoor pool and sauna), it has lost none of its rustic charm, and is very prettily furnished with a mixture of antiques and country prints. There's a good restaurant serving traditional classics, and its just 11km (7 miles) from the ski slopes of Baqueira Beret.

Calle Sortaus 9, Escunhau.
Tel: 973 64 00 48.

Hotel Niu dels Falcons ★★★

A chalet-style charmer in the ski resort of La

Molina, this is a good base for winter sports, or for hiking in summer. There are just seven rooms, set in forest, and with stunning views across the surrounding peaks. Home cooking is available in the pretty dining room.

Carrer Font Moreu 10, La Molina.
Tel: 972 89 20 73. www. niudelsfalcons-xalet.com

Hotel El Castell de Ciutat ★★★★

The ruins of the medieval castle of the Counts of Urgell have been incorporated into this luxurious hideaway, with glorious gardens, a pool, spa and gym. It's on the outskirts of La Seu d'Urgell and offers splendid views over the valley.

Carretera N260, Km 229, La Seu d'Urgell.
Tel: 973 35 00 00. www. hotel-castell-ciutat.com

Hotel Resguard dels Vents ★★★★

This chic rural hotel and spa is set in a green valley surrounded by lofty peaks. It offers special deals, offering beauty treatments and fine dining for a surprisingly modest price.

Camí de Ventaiola, Ribes de Freser.
Tel: 972 72 88 66.
www.hotelresguard.com

Hotel Torre del Remei ★★★★

A splendid Modernista *palacete* set in extensive gardens in the beautiful Cerdanya Valley, this is one of the most luxurious hotels in Northern Spain. The rooms are sumptuous, the restaurant outstanding, and the service immaculate.

Camí Reial, Bolvir de Cerdanya.
Tel: 972 14 01 82.
www.torredelremei.com

EATING OUT

El Galet ★

An old-fashioned, friendly spot on a pretty square in the middle of Puigcerdà's old quarter, this place specialises in grilled meats (*carns a la brasa*). Finish up with *crema catalana*, the Catalan version of crème brûlée.

Plaça Santa Maria 8, Puigcerdà.
Tel: 972 88 22 66.

Open: Wed–Mon.
Closed: Tue.

Els Caçadors ★

This modern but appealing hotel-restaurant in Ribes de Freser (the village from which the Cremallera railway creaks up to the Vall de Núria) is constantly packed. At weekends there are two or even three sittings, to accommodate the hordes of hungry walkers or skiers. Service is brisk and efficient, and the menu features hearty Catalan classics such as grilled meats cooked over charcoal. Plates are heaped high, and prices are exceptionally good.

Carrer Balandrau 24–26, Ribes de Freser.
Tel: 972 72 77 22.
www.hotelsderibes.com.
Open: daily for breakfast, lunch and dinner.
Closed: Nov.

Ca La Mary ★★

An exceptional country restaurant located in the mountain village of Queralbs, on the route up to the Vall de Núria. This is the place to come to try genuine Catalan

home cooking, but it can get hectic at weekends.
Carrer del Pla 21, Queralbs.
Tel: 972 72 73 77.

La Taverneta ★★
A delightfully old-fashioned country inn, this serves typical Catalan dishes such as *botifarra amb mongetes* (country sausage with beans) or lamb chops grilled over hot coals. It's a good place to fill up after a day's walking in the National Park of Aigüestortes.
Plaça Batllo, Boí.
Tel: 973 69 61 32.
Open: lunch & dinner.

Urtau ★★
A lively tapas bar serving *pintxos* (Basque-style tapas) with an adjoining dining room serving Basque-Navarrese cuisine.
Plaça Urtau 2, Arties.
Tel: 973 34 45 31.
Open: Thur–Tue lunch & dinner. Closed: Wed.

Borda Estevet ★★★
This old-fashioned stone *masía* (farmhouse) serves traditional mountain cuisine, including huge platters of grilled meats cooked over hot coals (*a la brasa*) and *trinxat*, a peasant dish made with mashed potatoes and vegetables topped with crispy bacon. Service is very friendly, if slow.
Carretera de la Comella 2, Andorra la Vella, Andorra.
Tel: 376 86 40 26.
www.bordaestevet.com

Fonda Xesc ★★★★
Appearances are deceptive at this traditional inn in the pretty mountain village of Gombrèn. The Fonda Xesc serves exceptional, contemporary Catalan cuisine, and offers delightful (reasonably priced) rooms.
Plaça del Roser 1, Gombrèn.
Tel: 972 73 04 04.
www.fondaxesc.com

Restaurant Sala ★★★★
The Catalans adore wild mushrooms (*bolets*), and no one does them better than Miquel Màrquez, the chef behind Sala. At any time of the year, the contemporary Catalan cuisine is a rare treat, but it's worth a special visit in autumn to try the outstanding *Menú del Bolet*.

Passeig de la Pau 27, Berga. Tel: 938 21 11 85.
Open: Tue–Sat lunch & dinner, Sun lunch only.
Closed: Mon.

Sport and leisure
Hípica Peufort
This riding school offers everything from short courses for beginners to week-long holidays for experienced riders.
Carrer Joaquin Sostres, Sort. Tel: 609 73 27 76.
www.hipicapeufort.es

Noguera Aventura
This adventure tourism company offers white-water rafting, canyon descent, mountain biking, hiking, snowbikes, horse riding and more.
Ciutat de Lleida, El Pont de Suert.
Tel: 973 69 00 55.
www.nogueraventura.com

Skiing
For Catalan ski resorts, including La Molina and La Masella, Baqueira-Beret, Vall de Núria and Boí Taüll, comprehensive information can be found at *www.catneu.net*. Full details of Andorra's ski resorts can be found at *www.skiandorra.ad*

Index

Acknowledgements

Thomas Cook Publishing wishes to thank CAROLINE JONES, to ~~~~ this book (except for the following images):

DREAMSTIME 58 (Francisco Javier Gil Oreja)
WIKIMEDIA COMMONS 56 (Ramessos)

For CAMBRIDGE PUBLISHING MANAGEMENT LTD:
Project editor: Karen Beaulah
Copy editor: Anne McGregor
Typesetter: Paul Queripel
Proofreader: Claire Boobbyer
Indexer: Karolin Thomas

SEND YOUR THOUGHTS TO
BOOKS@THOMASCOOK.COM

We're committed to providing the very best up-to-date information
our travel guides and constantly strive to make them as useful as they
can be. You can help us to improve future editions by letting us have
your feedback. If you've made a wonderful discovery on your travels
that we don't already feature, if you'd like to inform us about recent
changes to anything that we do include, or if you simply want to let us
know your thoughts about this guidebook and how we can make it even
better – we'd love to hear from you.

Send us ideas, discoveries and recommendations today and then look
out for your valuable input in the next edition of this title.

Emails to the above address, or letters to traveller guides Series Editor,
Thomas Cook Publishing, PO Box 227, Coningsby Road,
Peterborough PE3 8SB, UK.

Please don't forget to let us know which title your feedback refers